Take Authority over Autism

Conquering Autism Through the Power of God's Word

ANGELETTA GILES

© Copyright 2020—Angeletta Giles

All rights reserved. This book is protected by the copyright laws of the United States of America. This book may not be copied or reprinted for commercial gain or profit. The use of short quotations or occasional page copying for personal or group study is permitted and encouraged. Permission will be granted upon request. Unless otherwise identified, Scripture quotations are taken from the Easy-to-Read Version Copyright © 2006 by Bible League International Used by Permission. All rights reserved. Scripture quotations marked AMP are taken from the Amplified® Bible, Copyright © 2015 by The Lockman Foundation, La Habra, CA 90631. All rights reserved. Used by permission. Scripture quotations marked TPT are taken from The Passion Translation, Copyright © 2014, 2015, 2016, 2017, www.thepassiontranslation.com. Used by permission of BroadStreet Publishing Group, LLC, Racine, Wisconsin, USA. All rights reserved. Scripture quotations marked NCV are taken from The Holy Bible, New Century Version®. Copyright © 2005 by Thomas Nelson, Inc. All rights reserved. Scripture quotations marked MSG are taken from The Message. Copyright © 1993, 1994, 1995, 1996, 2000, 2001, 2002. Used by permission of NavPress Publishing Group. Scripture quotations marked NLT are taken from the Holy Bible, New Living Translation, copyright 1996, 2004, 2015. Used by permission of Tyndale House Publishers., Wheaton, Illinois 60189. All rights reserved. Scripture quotations marked NKJV are taken from the New King James Version. Copyright © 1982 by Thomas Nelson, Inc. Used by permission. All rights reserved. All emphasis within Scripture quotations is the author's own. Please note that Destiny Image's publishing style capitalizes certain pronouns in Scripture that refer to the Father, Son, and Holy Spirit, and may differ from some publishers' styles.

DESTINY IMAGE® PUBLISHERS, INC.
P.O. Box 310, Shippensburg, PA 17257-0310
"Promoting Inspired Lives."

This book and all other Destiny Image and Destiny Image Fiction books are available at Christian bookstores and distributors worldwide.

Cover design by Eileen Rockwell
Interior design by Terry Clifton

For more information on foreign distributors, call 717-532-3040.
Reach us on the Internet: www.destinyimage.com.

ISBN 13 TP: 978-0-7684-5167-2
ISBN 13 eBook: 978-0-7684-5168-9
ISBN 13 HC: 978-0-7684-5170-2
ISBN 13 LP: 978-0-7684-5169-6

For Worldwide Distribution.
1 2 3 4 5 6 7 8 / 24 23 22 21 20

Dedication

For every person who has ever prayed, encouraged, called, sent a text, private message, or commented on a social media post, insert your name here: _____. This book is dedicated to you.

Acknowledgments

Jesus, thank You for being You…Savior, Lord, and King. You call me friend. What a journey! I am so glad that I know You for myself. Growing up, I knew You through the lenses of others. I now know my own Jesus, and I am training Londyn to know You for herself. Thank You for our free, unfiltered relationship. You are my best Friend, and we have so much fun together.

Londyn, "my precious lamb": Words can't even express how much you mean to me. I love you, "Bun." You are my greatest gift after Jesus. I am so glad we get to do life together. I don't take this lightly: "I get to be your mom!"

"Thank you" to all of my family, work family, and friends. I tried to list every name, but I was afraid I would leave someone out.

I am living through the prayers of my great-grandmother, Matilda, my grandparents, and their siblings. Thank you all so much.

To #DemNaxes we have a bond that I would challenge any family to match. I love you.

Londyn has countless godmothers, special aunties and uncles, teachers, therapists, instructional aides, buddies, and friends. I praise God for allowing us to journey with you. We are so blessed to have you in our lives. Londyn especially wants to thank, "My family from Tennessee" (her words).

Thank you to:

Londyn's dad, Deitric and his family

My parents: Regina and Jennifer

My brothers and sisters: Amy, David, Nick, Junior, and Macee

Londyn's grandmothers: Regina, Frankie Mae, Jennifer, and Granny Irma

Londyn's great-granny: Minnie B.

Londyn's grandfather: James L.

Londyn's Un-Toya

My nieces and nephew: Kristyn, Grace, and Thatcher

My spiritual children: Jade, Terrin, and Alyssa

To Pastors Terry and Kim: I praise God for spiritual parents who have looked me in my eyes and proclaimed boldly and proudly, "I love you!" I know that these words are real, and Londyn and I get to experience them every time we are in your presence. Words cannot express our love for you, our elders, and our Impact Family. I thank God for placing us in a: *house of revival, house of discipleship, built around a culture of love.* Thank you for being pure examples of what love is.

Soul Gathering Ministries: Thank you for your foundational training on how to minister to souls. To my mom, Pastor Regina. What a great example of how to be a woman of authority and faith.

And to the Broadnax 3: Cookie, Candy, and David. We have a sibling bond that I (Cookie) praise God for every single day. I love you both more than you'll ever know.

To my first best friend, my grandmother Minnie B. I praise God for you and women like Aunt Susie who taught us how to pray.

Min. Ptorey, Mama Alberta, and the JesusGirl/GodsMan Praying Community: Thank you for reminding me that Londyn and I are answers to prayers. No doubt, your prayer calls were the catalyst for the manifestation of this book.

Pastor McCall: You and Londyn speak the same language. You have a special, unbreakable bond. Thank you for being an awesome children's pastor. Impact Children and Youth Department: Thank you to every pastor, leader, and volunteer. Thank you for sowing and equipping this generation.

Thank you to:

Don R. Roberts Elementary School and Forest Heights STEM Academy Staff

Staff at North Hills Services and Full Counsel Preparatory Center

Little Rock School District and the SPED Department, especially Cassandra, Sophia, and my god-mama "Miss Jo Anna"

Londyn's League of Extraordinary Doctors: Dr. Maya Lopez, Dr. Robert Choate, Dr. Bishawn Morris, Dr. Patrice Reed, Dr. Jayne Bellando. You have been more than clinicians, you are our family.

Londyn's classroom teachers from Pre-K to 5th grade: Ms. Doris, Ms. Cleo, Ms. Jane, Mrs. Glover, Mrs. Hendrix, Mrs. Alumbaugh, Mrs. Bradberry, Ms. McMichael, and Mrs. Jenkins

Londyn's IEP Dream Team: Ms. Downing, Mrs. Swindler, Dr. Loudermill, Mrs. Littrell, Mrs. Lovins, Mrs. Nixon, and Ms. Sims

All of our Volunteers and seed sowers for PAAK, #SuperMoms, #DunamisDads, #StrikeOutAutism, especially Mrs. Cindy and Pulaski Heights UMC, Michael "The Diaper Guy," and Dave and Tamara at Professor Bowl

Cheer City United, I CAN! of Arkansas, Reve Dance Academy, and Centre Stage Dance Academy: Because of you, Londyn and many other special athletes and overcomers have confidence and many trophies. Thank you for sowing your time and money for extracurricular activities just for them.

Andrea and the Arkansas Angels Pageant System volunteers and donors: Andrea, because you dared to ask for your crown, Londyn and many other princes and princesses have too many to count. We love you.

The Arkansas ATN: Maya, Jayne, Stefanie, Dawn, Teresa, and Suzanne; and our honorary FAB: Bob and our angels: Alma, Aulina, and Eldon

Angie and The Autism Treatment Network

Mentors: Gaby and Miss Virginia: Before I even knew I was an advocate, you poured into me and kept me encouraged. Thank you for always cheering me on!

Willa B: Thank you for proofing my proposal and manuscript from beginning to the end. You have an awesome gift and I cannot wait for the world to see what I see; and to Dana, thank you for staying up with me all night, giving me constant encouragement while I was writing.

Jeannie, Leah, Mandie, and Michaela: Words cannot express how much you mean to me. Thank you for sitting and reading with me in the ninth hour.

Amy from Cracker Barrel…you always allowed Londyn to pay. Even though her "credit card" didn't work, you took the time to "see" her as a paying customer.

Tina, Meelika, and Destiny Image Publishers: I thank you for partnering with us. Tina, I was able to email you morning, noon, or night and you were always encouraging. I praise God for you. Meelika, thank you for always being so sweet.

Cover photo: Katie Childs

Backcover photo: Jacob Slaton

Photo Hair stylists: Danyell Phillips and Venisha Brown

www.AutismOvercomers.com designed by Leta Joyner

I also want to thank the special people in my life who are now with Jesus: my Papa, Reverend Jim Cloman; my Broadnax Grandparents, Willie Mae and Fred; and my daddy, Bernard Broadnax Sr. Daddy, who named me "Cookie." I am grateful for the precious time that God allowed Londyn and I to have with you before you left. #DaddyWON

PRAYERS FOR ME AND LONDYN

The following are prayers I prayed and others prayed for me as I wrote this book. I believe God purposed me to write *Take Authority Over Autism* to help others seek Him while raising children diagnosed with autism.

> *"Please agree with me. I have locked myself in a hotel to finish my book. I want God's presence to overtake me in this room."* —Angeletta, 3/18/19

> *"Thank You, Jesus, for meeting Angeletta in a powerful way. Fill her heart and mind with Your words, anointed for Your purpose. Sweet Spirit, flow through her. We agree in Jesus' name!"* —Mona

> *"Yes! God, help her finish; quiet her mind so she can only hear You, Father God. Bless her with Your presence! May Jesus' blood be around her and her daughter while she works! Love you, girl, 100%! You, Father God, bring Your presence to cause Angeletta's mind to be directed by Your Spirit so she will share what You need her to say—transparent, real, heartfelt*

words that will give life to the parents who need You and Your touch for the race they are running.…" —BECCA

"Do it Lord! More in Jesus' name! Agreeing with you in Jesus' name! Father, thank You for a supernatural flow on Angeletta to finish the book You've given her! Divine productivity in Jesus' name!" —SHERRI

"Lord, let Your wisdom and knowledge rest upon Cookie and stir the creative ability to write afresh throughout this day." —MAMA

"Yes! Praying, Believing, Expecting, Receiving! God has this! Love, Hugs, Prayers!" —REV. BEV

"Keep your face set like a flint toward the One you love and serve. You know what He has called you to do. Blessings." —KIMBERLY

"I know that God is guiding you in this journey. You have such a beautiful perspective on autism and are a great mother. I pray that you receive all the praises you deserve through this project. Peace." —NICOLE

"Angeletta, your BIG servant's heart and Jesus-love amazes me! You are going to strike out autism all over this land." —PASTOR KIM

"Trust God's timing, you and Londyn will never be denied! Daddy always takes care of His girls. Because you are waiting in faith and you have a humble, servant heart, be prepared to receive far more that you have ever expected." —MAMA Z

"Come now, Holy Spirit. I surrender to Your complete control over my thoughts. Fill my heart. Consume me with Your fire." —ANGELETTA

CONTENTS

Foreword 1

Introduction   My Intercession for You 3

Chapter 1   Before We Can Overcome Together 11

Chapter 2   Identity Theft 21

Chapter 3   The Best Road Trip Ever 33

Chapter 4   Walk in Your Authority and Overcome 45

Chapter 5   Let's Start from the Beginning 61

Chapter 6   Adios Diagnose 73

Chapter 7   Overcome Speech 85

Chapter 8   Overcome Emotions 99

Chapter 9   Overcome Socialization and Relationships 111

Chapter 10   Overcome Behavior 123

Chapter 11   Overcome Learning 135

Chapter 12   Overcome Your Environments 151

Chapter 13   Encouragement for Caregivers, Family, Friends . 163

Glossary of Terms and Acronyms 177

About the Author 179

FOREWORD

Angeletta and Londyn have been part of our church family for many years—but more importantly, a major part of our lives. She has set an incredible example for me and this church body in faith, wisdom, kindness, and joy. She reminds me of what Paul told Timothy:

> *Be an example to the believers in word, in conduct, in love, in spirit, in faith, in purity. Till I come, give attention to reading, to exhortation, to doctrine. Do not neglect the gift that is in you, which was given to you by prophecy with the laying on of the hands of the eldership* (1 Timothy 4:12-14 NKJV).

Angeletta has walked before God as a mother challenged by a difficult diagnosis concerning her child, but has chosen to lift up her eyes to the hills from which comes her help; her help comes from the Lord. It is easy to believe God when all is going well and goals are being reached day by day. But when you have to wake up every morning and face a giant that says, "I am not moving," it is very different. I believe her victorious story has come because she has chosen to face each situation with her faith one day at a time. Her story is truly a journey of faith in a good God and her decision to thank God every day for her beautiful prize, Londyn.

I know I personally can't feel the hurt and pain you are facing when suddenly a doctor tells you that your child has autism. I have never walked that journey with a child. But what blesses me as a pastor is that God brings people into my life, and through relationship I am able to unite with them in their journey. Then I connect with their faith for God to do miracles. I am able to witness their steadfastness in God as they grab ahold of grace that manifests victory. That is what has happened in my relationship with Angeletta and Londyn. I hurt with them, and I also rejoice with them.

In her story, you will walk alongside her as she speaks over Londyn the words, "Honey, you're a genius" when Londyn could not form her words correctly. Now years later, Londyn looks at her mom and boldly says, "Mom, I'm a genius."

There are moments in their story when Angeletta has had her "Pull out a chair moment," when it was time for a face-to-face with God, her Father. Direction in our lives comes only from our Father who created us for His pleasure. As I read about her "God and chair moments," it really inspired me to do it myself. Wow! I sat down in my secret place and pulled a chair up for my Father. Politely I asked Him to be seated and then visualized Him sitting there talking to me. God's presence filled the room and I heard His voice clearer in that moment than I have heard in sometime. That revelation itself can change your life.

In this book you will be truly informed about how to lay your cares before the Lord while standing with the revelation that God is always good and He is good to your child. Healing will begin when you settle these issues in your heart and continue to read this beautiful testimony. I can say as Angeletta's pastor that she walks the walk and talks the talk. This book will inspire your heart through her laughter and tears—and will leave you filled with faith and hope. May the love of Jesus arise in your heart as you begin.

Pastor Terry Nance
Impact Church
Author, *God's Armorbearer*

MY INTERCESSION FOR YOU

Come now, Holy Spirit, let Your presence consume us.

JESUS, thank You for being here with this reader. As every person reads every word in this book, I want each one to feel Your presence. Your tangible presence. Where Your presence is there is freedom. I want readers to know You are with them. That You never have and You never will leave them. I want them to know that Your arm is long enough to reach them. That You are Abba, Father, and Daddy. I want them to know that not only did You give Your life for us, You also left a Person who lives inside us—the Spirit of God, the Holy Spirit. This is why You had to leave us so quickly, so that He could stay on earth. Because of this, we can be clothed with Your power. That same power will allow us to **take authority over autism.**

I want this reader and every reader to know that they are not alone. That I am going to be completely transparent about my struggles, hurts, disappointments, and most importantly, the victories over them. My promise is to introduce or remind them of hope—YOU! I speak to every distraction and hinderance while they are reading. They must go! Let them be consumed with Your love, Your joy, and Your peace. I want them to know that they cannot get enough of You. That You want them to come to You for everything, even when it seems so little and insignificant. You want them to know that everything that is a concern to them is a big deal to You. You love them so much. This book is not about me or Londyn. It is about a relationship with You!

Lord, throughout this book, this reader will take a huge leap of faith and list very specific prayer requests. Every prayer and request matters to You. I am so grateful that before we even ask, You have already answered. Let any fragments or memories of pain, abuse, and despair throughout this process be covered by Your blood. I want every reader to know that You are the God who heals. ***It is always Your will to heal!*** *I want them to know that they are preferred, that You would have died for them even if they were the only one. I want them to know that You selected them before they were formed in their mother's womb. I want them to know that they are Your favorite son or daughter. That You took this reader's place and would do it again in less than a second.*

I want every reader to know that although they will read our testimony and think that there must be something special about me and Londyn, there is something special about them as well. We are not the "lucky" ones, we have just tapped into our birthright power and authority, and from this point forward, they will tap into theirs. I know that they will think their situation is so stressful, and it must be Your will for them to remain like that. That "karma" controls their lives and there cannot possibly be a light at the end of the tunnel. That their child has autism or any other diagnosis, plain and simple. But...I am so excited that they will now have The Answer...You.

If whoever reads this book knows me personally or has heard of me, I want them to not be caught up in my written words, but to know that each word has been spoken by You, Lord, through me. These words were put into this book just for them. I want them to hear You speak directly to them. I know that the enemy's voice is loud, but Your voice is louder, Father. You are speaking to their hearts and any other voice is silenced.

We are ready, Lord because we have You! Amen.

ARE YOU READY?

Are you ready to take authority over autism? Say this out loud: "I am FREE. Lord, I trust You. You are with me while I am reading this book."

To take authority means to submit to His authority. You honor and submit by worshipping Him. Worship will increase your faith. How do you worship? By acknowledging that He is God, letting Him know how much you appreciate Him, and making Him your priority. I know you are worried about doing it right. The Holy Spirit is your greatest Teacher. Trust Him, He has wisdom for you as you complete the book. At the end of this chapter, there is a great Scripture in Psalms that will show you one way to worship Him.

Friend, throughout this process, you will be taking huge risks. You will be challenged in your thinking and pushed out of your comfort zone. Most importantly, for the first time, you will entertain the thought that your child *can* be healed of autism. While you are reading, I want you to know that we are on a journey together.

There will be moments when we will high-five each other in agreement to what I am saying. You are going to laugh. I hope you will laugh at me.

There will also be moments that will trigger deep hurt and painful reminders of what you or your child is going through. It may also trigger memories that you have experienced. Moments when you felt life was moving for everyone else except you. Moments when there was not one person you could call without getting their unsolicited advice and lecture on what they had not experienced personally. This book is not only for the individual or parent living with this diagnosis. It is for anyone impacted by autism, whether you are a teacher, caregiver, clinician, or friend. It is for anyone who wants to reclaim their birthright authority in every area of their lives.

Some readers may begin reading and say to themselves that there's nothing wrong with their lives. Even you may even believe that there is no need for you to overcome. Everything in your life is fine and you wouldn't change it. I want you to continue reading, because although the title specifically mentions autism, you will find that these same tools will apply and help you overcome in every area of your life.

We will talk about forgiveness: yourself, family, friends, and professionals. There will be moments when you won't get the opportunity to face someone who has wronged you. It is so important that you learn to forgive so that you can move on and overcome.

If you are someone who feels helpless because you cannot understand what the person closest to you is going through because of autism, this may trigger emotions for you as well. Please do not worry. The Holy Spirit carefully planned out these words for total healing. I speak to relationships. They will be restored!

Throughout this journey I have learned the power of transparency. When you release what is in your heart, the enemy cannot torment you or use it against you. When you release it to God, He will heal your heart. You cannot receive healing from what you will not admit. It is always His will to heal.

I will not hold anything back because we are in this together. I want you to do the same.

You will see pauses in my sentences where I say *breathe*. Please stop and do that. You may not know me personally to call me, but there is Someone who is waiting on your call and your prayers for understanding and healing. I want you to trust the process. There will be moments that you believe are insignificant, but they have made Londyn victorious.

Even as I am typing these words, Londyn and I have had some challenges. There were moments that seemed impossible to write in the midst of being overcomers. I laugh at myself because I had to come and read my own notes to remind myself that we are overcomers. I have had the privilege of ministering to parents all around the world, and yet, there were moments that I could not minister to myself. I am so glad that we are on this journey together.

As we embark on this wonderful experience together, I want you to learn how to ask God for anything. He has already promised to supply your needs (see Philippians 4:19). Faith is a muscle that must be exercised.

I dare you to ask God for something that seems unrealistic to what your human mind can contain. A year ago, I said that I would write a bestselling book, which seemed so unrealistic to me at the time. After I made my request to Him, I sat down at my laptop, and here we are. We have to get to the point where we have childlike faith. Londyn does not hesitate to ask for the most outrageous thing because in her mind, Mama will do it. We cannot even imagine what our BIG God wants to do for us, if we just ask.

Make your request—take the leap of faith! Say, "Thank You!" Rejoice, it is already done!

> *Lord, now that this reader has taken this huge step in faith by starting to read this book, I pray that Your healing power will be experienced. With each inhale and exhale, remind this precious friend that it is Your breath in his or her lungs—Your DNA and Your power.*

Are you ready to take authority?

SCRIPTURES TO STAND ON

Always make the Scriptures personal to you and your family. Confess them over yourself.

> *With Jesus as our high priest, we can feel free to come before God's throne where there is grace. There we receive mercy and kindness to help us when we need it* **(Hebrews 4:16)**.
>
> *I have told you these things, so that in Me you may have [perfect] peace. In the world you have tribulation and distress and suffering; but be courageous [be confident, be undaunted, be filled with joy]; I have overcome the world. [My conquest is accomplished, My victory abiding]* **(John 16:33 AMP)**.
>
> *But the person who trusts in the Lord will be blessed. The Lord will show him that he can be trusted. He will be strong, like a tree planted near water that sends its roots by a stream. It is not afraid when the days are hot; its leaves*

are always green. It does not worry in a year when no rain comes; it always produces fruit **(Jeremiah 17:7-8 NCV).**

I tell you this timeless truth: The person who follows me in faith, believing in me, will do the same mighty miracles that I do—even greater miracles than these because I go to be with my Father! For I will do whatever you ask me to do when you ask me in my name. And that is how the Son will show what the Father is really like and bring glory to him. Ask me anything in my name, and I will do it for you! **(John 14:12-14 TPT)**

The Lord is the Spirit, and where the Spirit of the Lord is, there is freedom **(2 Corinthians 3:17 NCV).**

I will answer them before they call for help. I will help them before they finish asking **(Isaiah 65:24).**

Let the whole world sing to the Lord! Tell the good news every day about how he saves us. Tell all the nations how wonderful he is! Tell people everywhere about the amazing things he does. The Lord is great and worthy of praise. He is more awesome than any of the "gods." All the "gods" in other nations are nothing but statues, but the Lord made the heavens! He lives in the presence of glory and honor. His Temple is a place of power and joy. Praise the Lord, all people of every nation; praise the Lord's glory and power! Give the Lord praise worthy of his glory. Come into his presence with your offerings. Worship the Lord in all his holy beauty. Everyone on earth should tremble before him! But the world stands firm and cannot be moved. Let the heavens rejoice and the earth be happy! Let people everywhere say, "The Lord rules!" **(1 Chronicles 16:23-31).**

A poetic song for thanksgiving. Lift up a great shout of joy to the Lord! Go ahead and do it—everyone, everywhere! As you serve him, be glad and worship him. Sing your way into his presence with joy! And realize what this really means—we have the privilege of worshiping the Lord our God. For he is our Creator and we belong to him. We are the people of his pleasure. You can pass through his open gates with the password of praise. Come right into his presence with thanksgiving. Come bring your thank offering to him and affectionately bless his beautiful name! For the Lord is always good and ready to receive you. He's so loving that it will amaze you—so kind that it will astound you! And he is famous for his faithfulness toward all. Everyone knows our God can be trusted, for he keeps his promises to every generation! **(Psalm 100 TPT)**

BEFORE WE CAN OVERCOME TOGETHER

Autism has a name, but there is no name greater than Jesus.

So God raised him up to the most important place and gave him the name that is greater than any other name (Philippians 2:9).

ARE YOU READY TO BE FREE?

Before we can move forward, you will have to believe or at least be willing to listen long enough as I share this important message from God. This may not be easy for you at first, but if you were at least willing to pick up the book and read it this far, please see it through. Please trust His process. He is with you.

God did not give your child autism! Autism is only a diagnosis; it is not in your child's DNA! It is not part of your child.

Autism is a lie from hell. God did not create it, and He is not punishing you by giving it to your child. He does not have to prove that He is God by making us vulnerable and helpless with disorders. A lie, a lie, a lie! He does not give us sicknesses or diseases to get our attention. Romans 8:31 says, *"If God is for us, no one can stand against us. And God is with us."*

Fill in the blanks and say this out loud: "God, You did not give _____ autism. God, You are not punishing me. You gave me _____ because You knew You could trust me with this child." Repeat this phrase daily until you know it without any doubt.

We must reprogram our thinking and how we have been operating. I had to do this too. It will not be easy. It will not happen overnight. It is a journey. It will take practice, but it is worth it. God is with you—knowing this is the key to you and your family's victory over autism. Even though I have put this in practice, I still correct myself. The Holy Spirit will help you change your thoughts and what you speak. He will remind you—but you must receive what He is saying. He is saying, *"I did not give your precious baby, My precious baby, autism."*

I love declaring Job 22:26-30 (MSG):

> *You'll take delight in God, the Mighty One, and look to him joyfully, boldly. You'll pray to him and he'll listen; he'll help you do what you've promised. You'll decide what you want and it will happen; your life will be bathed in light. To those who feel low you'll say, "Chin up! Be brave!" and God will save them. Yes, even the guilty will escape, escape through God's grace in your life.*

As the Scripture passage from Job 22 mentions, because you have *decided* that you have received healing for your precious child, it will happen. The journey ahead will take some shifting. It is important that you align yourself with people who also believe this. People who will support you in your belief of healing for your child. People who will speak this over your child. People who are in agreement with you. They will have to share the same mindset if they are to be in your corner.

You will get opposition and persecution for believing this. People will always have a problem or their own ideas. Choose to be like Jesus; when they persecute you, love them. Seeing those who are closest to you doubt what God has told you is one of the hardest things that I have had to deal with. I got through it! With the guidance of the Holy Spirit, I will show you how too.

What I have to share with you will be tough to take in. Autism has been the center of your life—I can relate. Through this diagnosis, you have made unique, long-lasting friendships, and you finally feel that your life has purpose because of it. A diagnosis is not your purpose. I am not saying that it has not been a path for great opportunities that have helped people. I just want you to shift your thinking like I had to. My platform should never keep anyone in bondage, but offer freedom through Jesus. After my great shift in mindset, I asked myself before participating in activities: Does it promote or introduce a relationship with Jesus? If those opportunities will not bring people closer to Jesus, I don't want to be part of them.

> Let's decree and declare: "God, I know without any doubt in my mind and heart that You want _____ healed of autism."

Now list everything that has come with the diagnosis, for example, speech delay, ADHD, etc.

There is no doubt in my mind that Londyn is healed! Jesus already died for it. He took her place. He literally had autism on the Cross. He defeated every sickness and disease. He bore it *all*. Isaiah 53:4-5 (NKJV) says:

> *Surely He has borne our griefs and carried our sorrows; yet we esteemed Him stricken, smitten by God, and afflicted. But He was wounded for our transgressions, He was bruised for our iniquities; the chastisement for our peace was upon Him, and by His stripes we are healed.*

> Let us decree and declare, "Lord, Your Word says that you bore all sickness and diseases. I decree and declare that _____ is healed of autism. _____ is healed because of Your stripes! I believe that You had stripes, therefore I believe _____ is healed."

Healing is a journey. Can God miraculously heal any disorder, sickness, or disease? Absolutely! He is God, and He can do anything. I have learned that the journey of healing is important, necessary, and absolutely worth it. Without taking the journey, Londyn and I would have missed the opportunities to see when God showed up and showed out in every situation, trial, and test, and when He stepped in and saved the day. The triumphs over the many obstacles taught us so much and prepared us to minister to you.

I know that you have been praying and praying to see change. There could be some things that are blocking you from receiving healing. That is why it is so important that you do the exercises at the end of the chapter. When you have the "Pull out the chair" moments, it will allow you to work through what is holding you back.

Some have asked, "God, even if You won't heal, can I at least see improvement?" I have asked God to bring revival to special-needs parents. I want the message of Jesus to supersede any message or awareness.

I love how Proverbs 12:25 (TPT) says, *"Anxious fear brings depression, but a life-giving word of encouragement can do wonders to restore joy to the heart."*

I want to give you a life-giving word of encouragement to restore joy in your heart. Being bound by fear is no longer an option. The broken record of anguish must go, especially since I know the Man who has already defeated it—Jesus.

I know you are waiting for change. Now, let us do it Jesus' way! Happy waiting, in joy waiting, in peace waiting, on vacation waiting, waiting with expectancy.

This book is very interactive. Faith is action, and the Holy Spirit wants you to partner with Him by reading every word and completing the exercises and homework. Also, read the Scriptures that conclude each chapter. His Word is our life source. We cannot live without it. When you read the Scriptures, ask the Holy Spirit for understanding, revelation, wisdom, and knowledge. Get a notebook, write down and date anything He shows you. Anything that you see, hear, or feel.

Now let's take authority. Declare this: "Jesus, I know that *now faith* comes by hearing the Word of God. Jesus, I have heard Your Word in Philippians 2:9-10, and I exercise my NOW faith. Jesus, Your Word says that there is no name greater than Your name and autism has a name. Autism, I use my authority against you by the Word of God! Autism, BOW DOWN!"

Matthew 28:18 (AMP) tells us that: *"Jesus came up and said to them, 'All authority (all power of absolute rule) in heaven and on earth has been given to Me.'"*

Write this as big as you can: GOD DID NOT GIVE _____ AUTISM! I AM NOT BEING PUNISHED FOR MY PAST SINS. JESUS HAS ALREADY PAID FOR THEM! Feel free to add anything else that is on your heart right in this very moment.

_____

_____

_____

_____

I am in agreement with you! Look at what Jesus says in Matthew 18:19 (NLT) *"I also tell you this: If two of you agree here on earth concerning anything you ask, my Father in heaven will do it for you."* You and I make two!

Say this until you believe it with all your heart: "God, I believe that You did not give my child autism! Jesus' name is above every name. I can't even comprehend the magnitude and the power of that name, Jesus...what a gift! I stand on Your name; I fight, sit, bow to Your name. I take authority through the power of Your name!"

You have to say it to take authority over it. By saying it, I did not allow autism to take authority over me or Londyn. I pray you will do the same. This may take some time, but until you can detach from the thought that God gave this to your child, then you won't be able to receive His victory and healing in your life. Continue to say it and teach your child how to say it too. If your child is pre-verbal, put it on his or her assistive technology device or record it where your child can hear it playing over and over. Even if your child is unable to form the words yet, his or her sharp brain is processing the declaration over his or her life.

Record the following confession and play it daily. It can be played while your child is getting ready for school or on the ride to school or during bath time. Anytime and as many times of the day as you like. Londyn began to memorize it. I would rather her repeat this during her echolalia versus a silly cartoon.

> God, You did not give _____ autism. _____ belongs to You and has Your DNA. I denounce autism as having control over our lives. You have control over our lives. Autism has a name and there is no name greater than the name of Jesus. I take authority over autism now. Autism, bow down. God is in control over our lives. Our identity is in Him, and not you. _____ is healed because Jesus made sure autism was defeated on the Cross.

FAITH IN ACTION

Choose a spot in your home that will be *the spot* where you will talk to God throughout this process and afterward. It can be a closet, favorite chair, or if you're like me, a particular spot on your couch. You can most certainly talk to God *anywhere* and *anytime*, but this will be your *favorite spot* where you will do most of your talking.

Become involved with a community of believers. I love and believe in the local church. I have fellowship with many wonderful people in a variety of places, and I understand that there are new ways of coming together through small groups, home groups, and Bible studies. The Holy Spirit will lead you, so please find a place and attend regularly. Jesus was always with a community of believers. More importantly, your children need a spiritual authority in their lives in addition to you. Over the past year, Londyn's children's pastor, Pastor McCall, has been very instrumental in my decision making. She was able to help me see things when my judgments were clouded.

PULL OUT A CHAIR

The devil is always trying to prove God is a liar. It is his job. Think about Eve in the Garden of Eden (Genesis 3:1). His weapon of deception was, "Did God really say that?"

I want you to take two chairs and face them together. I want you to sit in one and invite God to sit in the other. It is time for you to release was has been hidden in your heart. He wants you to give it *all* to Him. Every word, hurt, pain, disappointment. He's been waiting to have this intimate conversation with you. He is a big

God. So what if it doesn't make sense to you or profanity slips. He is not offended by it. Talk to Him. Yell at Him.

When I did this the very first time a few years back, I realized God was waiting. When I trusted Him enough to give Him the ugly, He was able to move in my life freely—but I had to first release everything to Him. Guess what, He will not tell anyone!

Write down your thoughts.

SCRIPTURES TO STAND ON

But the Lord said, "My grace is all you need. Only when you are weak can everything be done completely by my power." So I will gladly boast about my weaknesses. Then Christ's power can stay in me. Yes, I am glad to have weaknesses if they are for Christ. I am glad to be insulted and have hard times. I am glad when I am persecuted and have problems, because it is when I am weak that I am really strong **(2 Corinthians 12:9-10)**.

Now my beloved ones, I have saved these most important truths for last: Be supernaturally infused with strength through your life-union with the Lord Jesus. Stand victorious with the force of his explosive power flowing in and through you **(Ephesians 6:10 TPT)**.

So if the Son sets you free from sin, then become a true son and be unquestionably free! **(John 8:36 TPT)**

You will also decide and decree a thing, and it shall be established for you; and the light [of God's favor] will shine upon your ways **(Job 22:28 AMP)**.

He must become more and more important, and I must become less important **(John 3:30)**.

Therefore, God elevated him to the place of highest honor and gave him the name above all other names, that at the name of Jesus every knee should bow, in heaven and on earth and under the earth **(Philippians 2:9-10 NLT)**.

Listen well to wise counsel and be willing to learn from correction so that by the end of your life you'll be known for your wisdom **(Proverbs 19:20 TPT)**.

For here is eternal truth: When that time comes you won't need to ask me for anything, but instead you will go directly to the Father and ask him for anything you desire and he will give it to you, because of your relationship with me. Until now you've not been bold enough to ask the Father for a single thing in my name, but now you can ask, and keep on asking him! And you can be sure that you'll receive what you ask for, and your joy will have no limits! **(John 16:23-24 TPT)**

If you, imperfect as you are, know how to lovingly take care of your children and give them what's best, how much more ready is your heavenly Father to give wonderful gifts to those who ask him? **(Matthew 7:11 TPT)**

IDENTITY THEFT

You and your overcomer say the following out loud. If your overcomer is preverbal, please record this on their assistive technology device: "My identity is not in autism. My identity is not in any diagnosis. My identity is in Jesus."

I want to start off by thanking God for His grace. Prior to receiving the revelation of our identity, I wore my daughter's diagnosis of autism as a badge of honor. My life was consumed by it. It took priority in my life and was dictating our purpose. I even believed that because of it, I finally knew who I was and my purpose, as if autism was my creator. Through spending time with the Holy Spirit, He lovingly told me to shift my focus from living an autism-focused life to living a Jesus-focused life. The truth is, you cannot live by both. God's heart is to lead you to your rightful place; who you are, where He is.

As we begin our journey together, this chapter is so important. It was my favorite part of writing our love story to you. It has been easy to live it, but not so easy to share God's heart concerning autism. When I first shared my revelation on social media, I got a lot of backlash and persecution. The enemy wants you to believe that I am ashamed of my daughter, or I have not accepted her the way she is. I am here to tell you that Londyn is made in the image of God. *That* is the way she is. Genesis 1:27 (NKJV) says, *"So God created man in His own image; in the image of God He created him; male and female He created them."*

We are not created in the image of our diagnosis or circumstances. We are created in the image of God. Anything contrary to God, we will not accept.

So, as you are reading throughout the book, I want you to remember this. The enemy wants us to identify with anything but God. When we begin to recognize who we are and walk in our birthright authority, his attacks are powerless. When I realized that our ministry was not only overcoming autism but also coming against identity theft, there were many who resented me. The identity thief wants to misconstrue my words. He wants you to believe that speaking against the diagnosis will show others that you are ashamed of your child. I am not attacking someone you love or who is dear to you. I am attacking the autism diagnosis.

Therefore, in this moment, you must separate the two. If you don't, then every time I speak to the diagnosis of autism, you will take it personally. You will hear me speaking against your child and that is *not* what I am doing. You may have even been offended by the book title: *Take Authority Over Autism*. You probably asked, "Is that even possible?" Or, "Why are you trying to change your daughter?" Or, "Different not less." Londyn is absolutely different and not less, but that is not because of her diagnosis. It is because the same power that raised Jesus from the grave lives in her.

Take a moment and say this out loud: "Father, I am releasing my identity from autism. I give it back to you." Repeat this and add anything else that has consumed your identity.

I am not judging you for your actions. Remember, before this revelation and reality check I was there too. Now I am judging the one who since the beginning of time has lied to us. The evil one knows that he is defeated. His only weapon is to distract us away from our true identity. He is the accuser of believers, so his job is to always remind you that you are not worthy of forgiveness, healing, or standing in your inheritance as a child of God.

I want you to see Jesus before you see a diagnosis. Why do you think the identity thief steals identities? He wishes he could be like you. If he can get you to believe that you belong to something else and that something else takes attention away from God, then you will be distracted from living out your purpose.

Receiving a diagnosis is not a blessing in disguise. So why does your child have it? Why did Londyn have it? How would we know that we could just touch the hem of Jesus' garment if it were not for the woman with the issue of blood? (See Luke 8:43-48.) How would we know that blind eyes could see without the man who was born blind? (See John 9:1-7.) And we learn from Hannah who stayed in prayer until her promise came. (See First Samuel 1:9-20.) I am here to tell you that autism is no different! We overcome by the words of our testimony (Revelation 12:11). You are an autism overcomer because you believe in the God who honors His Word above His name (Psalm 138:2).

God writes Londyn's future. I don't have to wear autism as badge of honor, but I can take our journey and use it for His glory. Our kids are special because they are created in the image of Christ, not in the image of autism. Our identity in Christ has to be more valuable than the identity that is given by the world. The world sorts us by culture, class, and so on. At any given moment it decides if you aren't in the right category.

In Christ's identity there is no rejection. It is easy to get rejected by people if you don't meet their standards. This was so true for me and Londyn. When Londyn was first diagnosed, she was not autistic enough. I remember people saying, "So where did you get diagnosed?" "Did she get the 299 diagnosis? Really? Are you sure? She just doesn't look autistic." That is really when the revelation hit home. She is not supposed to look autistic. She is created in the image of God. She is supposed to look like Him. In His identity, there is no rejection!

I am so glad that we received the revelation about our identity being in Christ and not in autism.

Identity theft takes us from our Kingdom position. What is the solution to protect yourself from this happening? Right now, on the market there are several resources that you can set in place to protect your identity from identity theft. There are safeguards that can even be added to your credit reports. I am here to offer you a *free* identity protection program. It is a personal relationship with Jesus. You may ask, "Angeletta, how do I get it?" Pray this prayer: "Jesus, please give me a revelation of who You are. I want to know more about You. I want a relationship with You."

At the end of the chapter, there is a prayer that will take you a step further.

Let me emphasize the word *personal*. Prayer is your private, intimate connection between you and Jesus. Therefore no one can give you any opinion about it outside of His Word. He is better than a best friend. My conversations and relationship with Him are no different from my relationship with my besties. I can talk to Him about anything in any way. I said no to religion and yes to a relationship. I know that may be hard for you to grasp and understand. I want you to be free. He wants you to be free.

I love talking to Jesus especially now that I know there is no formality. Growing up I thought that there had to be a grand performance to talk to God. I thought my body had to be positioned a certain way. I thought it had to be a particular time of the day. I thought it had to be in a special place. Now I know that when He said we have access to His throne, He meant it. He told me that He does not want me to be open and relaxed when I talk to one of my friends yet come to Him guarded, withdrawn, and secretive. I was too busy trying to be formal, finding the right place, right time, and the right posture to talk to Him. I was wasting time that could have be spent with Him.

You may have prayed a prayer like this, "Lord, I know I should be running to You, but I don't feel like I get any answers. Actually, if I am going to be real with You, it is easier to make a call and get a response; although the person on the other end of the line may not have the wisdom that I need."

Guess what? God is a big God, and He can take it. As a matter of fact, He wants it. When we come to Him just as we are and not wrapped in the most beautiful paper with a big faux bow, He is able to really move in our life. Religion has conditioned us to try and fix ourselves a little bit, then go to Him. Stop what you're doing and go to Him right now. If you don't know what to say, start with, "Jesus, help." This is Londyn's favorite prayer. When she comes home and talks to me about an obstacle or concern at school, I always tell her to start with, "Jesus, help."

A simple prayer can look like this: "I don't feel like praying, Lord. I'm weak."

His response: *"My grace is enough for you. When you are weak, my power is made perfect in you"* (2 Corinthians 12:9 NCV). There are special rights and privileges when you accept your identity in Christ. You get to tap into His perfect power.

ARE THEY REALLY SAVED?

I have had several parents ask me about my thoughts on their children's salvation. It is this simple—Psalm 127. Remember, salvation is based on the child's personal relationship with Jesus. Our sweet, sweet Savior loves your children. Whether you believe they understand or not, your responsibility is to introduce them to Christ. He will take care of the rest. I love hearing Londyn's reaction when she feels God's presence. Wow—those moments I will always cherish.

The following is a social media response that I left for a parent who posed the question: *Are they really saved?*

> Wow, what a wonderful, transparent moment. I'm not at all saying this is THE answer, but here is how I found peace. Scripture teaches us that He knows every single hair on our heads and that we are made in His Image. So, as Londyn's mom, I am to train her and set the example. When I don't understand how, or simply can't get Londyn to understand, I say, "Lord, clarify anything to Londyn that I can't explain. Visit her in her dreams, send ministering angels." In this scenario, our faith is what's tested, not theirs. We have to trust God that He will reveal what we simply can't. I have also had to tell a crying dad that our precious Savior knows His beautiful creations and would never hold anything against them for lack of understanding. Londyn is very high functioning, matter of fact, and literal. When I get stuck explaining, I look up and say, "Lord, Your turn." lolololol I've also trained her to pray for understanding for herself. The most important thing is to train them to seek God for themselves, whether they

understand or not what that is. With our faith like Hannah's, we have to give them back to Him and trust Him to be their Savior, Teacher, Redeemer... P.S., all of this is in my book.

I want to share a funny moment that I had with Jesus a few years back.

Londyn knows all about Jesus and has asked Him to come into her heart. Someone asked me why Londyn had not been baptized yet. "You need to hurry. She is getting too old. Aren't you concerned about her salvation?" Their words concerned me, thus bringing fear and doubt to my mind. I was talking to Jesus about it and He told me this, "The next time someone says Londyn is getting too old, tell them I was thirty when I got baptized!" Talk about a mic-drop moment!

Londyn has known about Jesus since being in my womb. Do you really think He has His arms folded in disappointment toward us because she has not been baptized yet? Have faith, my friends! Tell your overcomer all about Jesus. Ask God to show you a wonderful pastor who can also lead them, and He will take care of the rest. She will definitely be baptized and it will not be because I made her. It will be because she made the decision. Spend time with Him. The same Man who flipped over tables in His Father's house will rescue you!

By resisting identity theft, I am prepared for Londyn's transition into adulthood. We still have a few years until that time comes, but the Holy Spirit is already training me. He showed me a few years back that adulthood is not something that you begin training for when children are approaching the age. You start now. I know society has set the age of adulthood at 18. At 18, even typical individuals are forced into adulthood, which most are not prepared for.

God told me that I am to release my authority over Londyn when He instructs me. Ask the Holy Spirit to give you a glimpse of your child's future and start cultivating it. If you see a future in technology, allow him or her to join a club at school or enroll your child in a technology school.

When I asked God for a glimpse of Londyn's future, He told me about her personality and strong will. He has shown me how to train her to set boundaries. I want her to follow God, His voice, and be sensitive to His instructions. Most importantly, I have to move out of His way! She can come to me for prayer and confirmation, but I need to honor her obedience to Him, even when I think she should be doing it a different way.

She can also pray and ask God to show her spiritual mentors. There is no junior Holy Spirit. There is only one Holy Spirit. The time to train your child is now. Whether your child is high-functioning or severe, your journey of healing will begin when you focus on your child's purpose—not his or her circumstance. If you have led them to Jesus, there is a big Holy Spirit living inside them. With Him comes spiritual gifts just waiting to be used for His Kingdom.

NOW TAKE AUTHORITY

Take the weight off of yourself—Jesus always intended to carry it. You can try to carry it, but He can and will go places that you will never be able to reach. Give your child back to the Lord right now. Have your own dedication service in his or her bedroom. Say this:

> Lord, _____ is Your child, the one You love most. What I can do in my own might is limited. With You in charge, it is limitless. I give _____ back to

you. By the power and authority that is mine through Jesus Christ, autism GO! You have no place here. My identity is in Jesus, not in a diagnosis. The world has perverted our right to speak against what is not of God. I am speaking against you autism, not _____. I am speaking against a diagnosis that wants to overcome us. It is trying to win over our God-given identity, but it cannot have us. I take authority over fear! Now that I have received my identity in Jesus, fear go!

My prayer for you:

I rebuke every lie the enemy has told you. Your identity is in Christ alone and not autism or anything else. I command that you will begin to see things through His eyes. I command authority over every cell, tissue, organ, and organ system in this reader's child's body. They must line up according to Your Word. We serve a supernatural God who operates beyond what is natural. You will live your life fearlessly. You will enjoy every freedom in Christ.

FAITH IN ACTION

Now that your child has taken on the identity of Jesus and not autism, allow him or her to try something new that is the opposite of autism. This will crush the back of fear. That is what life is all about, learning, even from mistakes. Watch your words. There is life and death in the power of your tongue. For example, I do not say that Londyn is autistic. That is allowing identity theft. I say, Londyn was diagnosed with autism and is walking in her healing.

For preverbal overcomers, utilize an assistive technology device so they can decree and declare Scriptures on their own.

I want you to take a moment and look in a mirror. Now, I want you to look your child in their eyes and say this out loud:

> *Oh yes, you shaped me first inside, then out; you formed me in my mother's womb. I thank you, High God—you're breathtaking! Body and soul, I am marvelously made! I worship in adoration—what a creation! You know me inside and out, you know every bone in my body; you know exactly how I was made, bit by bit, how I was sculpted from nothing into something. Like an open book, you watched me grow from conception to birth; all the stages of my life were spread out before you, the days of my life all prepared before I'd even lived one day* (Psalm 139:13-16 MSG).

What are you feeling right now? Write about it.

_____

_____

_____

_____

_____

ACTIVATING MY PERSONAL IDENTITY THEFT PROTECTION

My truth moment: I told Jesus that I felt so alone, forgotten, and abandoned because I was divorced and a single mom. I asked Him, "Do You care about single moms?" He said loudly, yet so gentle, "Of course I do! My mom was alone, forgotten, abandoned, and single until Joseph was visited by Gabriel (Matthew 1:19-29). I am always with you."

I will not allow *single mom* to steal my identity. I have the best Husband ever; just as Isaiah 54:5 says, *"Your real husband is the one who made you. His name is the Lord All-Powerful. The Holy One of Israel is your Protector, and He is the God of all the earth!"*

My reward for waiting until His perfect timing will be great.

SCRIPTURES TO STAND ON AND THE PRAYER OF SALVATION

Now that you have a revelation of who Jesus is, would you like to be part of His family? Pray this prayer:

> *Jesus, I now have a revelation of who You are. You are the Son of God. You died on the Cross for all of my sins, and You rose from the grave. I believe with all of my heart that You are alive today! I want You alive in me! I want You to save me now. I want to be part of Your family. Forgive me of all of my sins. Thank You, Jesus, I receive Your grace.*

Welcome to the family! Angels, Londyn, and I celebrate with you. I am so glad that everyone will have the opportunity to know Jesus.

> *Trust in the Lord completely, and do not rely on your own opinions. With all your heart rely on him to guide you, and he will lead you in every decision you make. Become intimate with him in whatever you do, and he will lead you wherever you go* **(Proverbs 3:5-6 TPT)**.
>
> *Children are God's love-gift; they are heaven's generous reward* **(Psalm 127:3 TPT)**.

"So no weapon that is used against you will defeat you. You will show that those who speak against you are wrong. These are the good things my servants receive. Their victory comes from me," says the Lord **(Isaiah 54:17 NCV)**.

What you say can mean life or death. Those who speak with care will be rewarded **(Proverbs 18:21 NCV)**.

I will worship toward Your holy temple, and praise Your name for Your lovingkindness and Your truth; for You have magnified Your word above all Your name **(Psalm 138:2 NKJV)**.

Whenever my busy thoughts were out of control, the soothing comfort of your presence calmed me down and overwhelmed me with delight **(Psalm 94:19 TPT)**.

You didn't choose me, but I've chosen and commissioned you to go into the world to bear fruit. And your fruit will last, because whatever you ask of my Father, for my sake, he will give it to you! **(John 15:16 TPT)**

THE BEST ROAD TRIP EVER

I don't know the scientific definition of autism because my mom told me that I belong to Jesus and not to a disorder...I don't even know what a disorder is.

—LONDYN, *age 10*

How are you? I know the previous chapter was intense. I believe we do not want to boldly say that our child is healed of autism because of fear. Fear of the next meltdown, of how they still process information, or are stimming, or literally cannot speak. For now, reread the previous chapters over and over again until you can read further.

Before you can overcome, you have to start at one. Do you agree that God did not give your child autism? If not, write down what you are struggling with. If you are already in agreement, take a moment and write a thank-you note to God.

Truth moment. If you believe God gave children, your child, autism, then the journey of healing will not come easy. In fact, most will never be able to receive the healing because they believe that is the way they are supposed to be.

Society has tried to downplay our freedom to trust and serve our mighty God. To stand boldly and profess the powerful name of Jesus is perceived as outdated and out of touch with reality. We are told we are not practical enough when we would rather wait on Him with the promise of renewed strength. We are constantly reminded that our faith is unrealistic.

The only way you are going to be able to overcome autism is to put the name of Jesus above it. You can do this by getting to know Him. Not *of* Him, but an intimate relationship where you share all of your ugly secrets and receive His love. Be patient with the process. I do not want you to read the first chapter and think that this is far above your head. The Holy Spirit carefully wrote this out for me and you. We will get through it and have the life He wants us to live.

"Angeletta, I believe in God, but I don't know how to have a relationship with Him."

How did you get to know your best friend or spouse? You talked to them. Shared experiences. Spent time together. It is the same with Jesus. You have complete access into His life by reading His Word. You pull out a chair and talk to Him, but allow Him the opportunity to talk back.

It is also important that you share this with your overcomer. Train up children in the way they should go (Proverbs 22:6). There is a promise with that Scripture. When they are old, they will not depart. They must know Jesus. He can reach places that we cannot, diagnosis or not.

You and I are officially on a road trip. We are about to embark on a journey that will be most memorable. I know that you would not just go on a journey with me without knowing me. That is why I took time to really open my heart and be vulnerable to you in the previous chapters. Buckle up. There will definitely be lots of pit stops, wrong turns, re-routings, and so forth. Are you all set? Are you ready to get on the road? Wait! There is another passenger who would really like to go with us. I do not want to go without Him, and honestly, we cannot.

I want to share my contribution to the *Book of Hope*:

> Singled out. In the span of one year (2012), my marriage was failing, and my daughter was diagnosed with autism. I became a special-needs mom and a single mom, all at once! Talk about a major adjustment! We'd never experienced autism in my family, and I found myself reaching out to any and all support that was available. The initial problem was, I felt singled out in support groups as well. My daughter was usually the only girl with autism and the only minority. I found that my stories were never relatable…so I thought. It finally occurred to me that in our "autism world" there is uniqueness, but also, we have

a common bond. We are all traveling in this journey of autism.

Along this journey, we will somehow come across the same forks in the road, bumps, sharp curves and turns, but we'll get through it, together! I always encourage new families that I am fortunate to meet along the way to see this journey as a road trip. Who would be the one person or people you'd take with you for the ultimate road trip? Invite this person on this autism road trip with you. They will choose to "get it" when you make unfavorable decisions that work best for your child. They are available as a sounding board, a crying shoulder, or will supply the rocks when throwing them is needed. Most importantly, they will stand with you when you are calming down a meltdown that refuses to be calmed down. I found my road trip crew and I'm no longer singled out.

I really was singled out. My first experience with the special-needs community was not a pleasant one. Londyn and I did not fit "the look." I can understand why—we looked like Jesus. We refused to honor what did not create us or take care of us.

On road trips you tell each other secrets that you are ashamed to repeat. The secrets cripple your thoughts and burst out with the hope for someone to relate and offer answers. This journey has been very isolating. There were times when my guard was always up. I felt like I had to fight.

I had to find people who at least could relate. I was grateful for family and friends who could share experiences, but their experiences were not their own personal experiences as a parent. "I am a mom, only a mom could relate. My experience was going to be different from a dad's experience." When couples call, the first thing that I want them to realize is women and men are going to react differently. Just because their reaction was not as dramatic as yours does not make their love less.

After the diagnosis, it is so important that you do not remain hidden. Come out and find your people. In overcoming anything, you cannot do it alone. God did not design us that way. Even Jesus had His peeps with Him throughout His journey and only took time away to fast and pray and spend time with His Father. As I mentioned, your people will "choose to get it."

As you read each chapter, I cannot wait to share with you some of the lifelong relationships that I have gained during our road trip. These wonderful people are now our family. It has been a blast, and I am excited about our future destinations. I must add that it is alright if they are not related to you.

One of the hardest realities I have faced on this journey is realizing that sometimes there are people who cannot go with you. We often force it, but it was not meant to be and there are several factors. Some do not have the capacity. Some outright refuse. I know you have been persecuted, but pray for them. Do not stay in offense. God is skilled in divine connections. Wait on Him. Trust me, we all need a "sent one" straight from God. Over the years I have been blessed with many unlikely friendships.

As we are on this road trip together, we will hold each other accountable and pray in faith. Most importantly we will have the Holy Spirit to guide us.

"But Angeletta, we have prayed and prayed and my child is now thirty and he still has severe autism."

I want to encourage you to not pray because of your circumstance or focusing on your circumstance—rather, pray like you and your child already have the victory. See your son or daughter the way God sees them. Here is an example of one of my favorite conversations with a mom who recently received the diagnosis:

> If you do not believe in your child and you are his mommy, then no one will. I know that he cannot talk now, but do you believe that someday he will? Then start acting like that day is today. Is your child the most wonderful human being that you have ever met? Then treat him that way. Treat him like he is a future president, magnificent teacher, or entrepreneur. As long as you see him as handicap, you will treat him like a handicap. You will respond to him like a handicap. Not only will you do it, but others will follow your lead.

There are some people you will pick up to go on the trip with you, but along the way, they will decide they do not want to go. There are some who will start, but you will have to drop them off somewhere. I have found on this journey that some people will come before I ask them, and some will always have an excuse. That is why we should always seek God before we go anywhere with anyone. There are some who really want to go, but they are not prepared. The journey costs too much. In my case, God allowed some people on the journey to teach and reveal to me something about myself. For those you have had to, or will need to leave behind, pray for them. Love them.

As we go on this journey together, I want you to remember Psalm 27:14 (TPT):

Here's what I've learned through it all: Don't give up; don't be impatient; be entwined as one with the Lord. Be brave and courageous, and never lose hope. Yes, keep on waiting—for he will never disappoint you!

When I meet people, I do not want them to leave me or to have spoken to me with only "autism" in common. I want them to experience Jesus. I want to be His hands and feet more than as an autism advocate. I am not saying that it is impossible to do both. The difference is, I have a Jesus agenda, not an autism agenda. I want you to know that there is something special about us because I know Jesus, not because I am a mom of a child with an autism diagnosis.

The following is a post that I wrote:

> TESTimony! Since last week, I have been fighting for Londyn's benefits. Countless 1-800 reps, face-to-face meetings, and I couldn't get anywhere. In most cases, the rep really didn't care, but I kept proclaiming that God is in control of our lives...He is for us! They "think" they have the control, but God is always ahead. So today I decided I'd go back downtown and hopefully get a rep who would listen before already deciding to turn me down. NOTHING is by accident. While waiting to advocate for Londyn, I had the privilege of ministering Jesus to a soul! My heart is full! To get an opportunity to lead a soul to Christ is worth what I've been going through. He left thanking me continuously, and I was still waiting to be called back. Forty minutes later as I was getting ready to leave, someone walked up to me and said, "God told me to empty my wallet for you...!" My God is...

That is what is most important, being a soul winner! He will take care of the rest.

No matter what, trust Him; it is going to work out for your good. One thing that I am sure of is even when Londyn could not form words or complete sentences, I knew that she understood me. I could see it in her eyes. She is a genius. To this day and forever, she says to me, "Mama, I'm a genius." That is because I told her she was. Friend, your child will be what you call him or her. I know she has a diagnosis, but I call Londyn an overcomer. I call her healed. I call her a genius. Her name is victory.

FAITH IN ACTION

Are you ready for the ultimate road trip? The most important characteristic of great road trip buddies is that they will openly pray with you. Who are your prayer partners? Who would you take with you on this journey? Write their name(s) below.

_____

_____

_____

_____

_____

If you cannot think of anyone, say this out loud, "God, who can I take with us on this road trip?" Don't force it, He will show you the right person or people. If you already have your peeps, call them and say thank you!

_____

_____

_____

Just in case you are wondering, yes, you need a road trip buddy. You cannot develop an us-against-the-world mentality. Jesus wants you in relationships.

Share any decisions with your road trip buddy before doing anything. Try not to be reactive even if you feel justified in your response. Your road trip buddy will always encourage you to seek the Holy Spirit before making a decision. Your buddy will also pray with you.

Share social media posts so you can encourage others. We overcome by the words of our testimony (Revelation 12:11). Believe me, He does not want to remain anonymous.

Remember, your way is not working. Let me keep it real on this road trip. Your way will never work. Parenting in your own understanding will lead to destruction. Your focus may be on a simple distraction while missing what God needs you to be warring against. Search your heart for the desire to be right, while not wanting to lose the control. What is best for your overcomer is not always what you think is best. Accept when you are wrong—it's okay. God is not mad at you—He's madly in love with you.

Stop looking at your circumstance, look at Jesus. The more you are focused on it and not Him, the less you are achieving your victory and peace.

PULL OUT A CHAIR

The following is one of my *pull out a chair* moments:

Uh God, my bargaining chip about writing this book is this—if I am going to write a book about overcoming autism, overcoming obstacles, overcoming "delayed" promises, and overcoming fears, then about the time I turn my manuscript in, which is August 17, 2019, every prayer would need to be answered, clarified, and I will need to see some light.

P.S. Every prayer request has already been answered!

Your turn! Write your prayer requests:

_____

_____

_____

_____

_____

_____

SCRIPTURES TO STAND ON

I will give them a heart to know Me [understanding fully] that I am the Lord; and they will be My people, and I will be their God, for they will return to Me with their whole heart **(Jeremiah 24:7 AMP).**

Never stop praying **(1 Thessalonians 5:17).**

But as the Scriptures say, "No one has ever seen, no one has ever heard, no one has ever imagined what God has prepared for those who love him." **(1 Corinthians 2:9).**

But the Helper will teach you everything and cause you to remember all that I told you. This Helper is the Holy Spirit that the Father will send in my name. I leave you peace. It is my own peace I give you. I give you peace in a different way than the world does. So don't be troubled. Don't be afraid **(John 14:26-27).**

A joyful, cheerful heart brings healing to both body and soul. But the one whose heart is crushed struggles with sickness and depression **(Proverbs 17:22 TPT).**

Are you weary, carrying a heavy burden? Then come to me. I will refresh your life, for I am your oasis. Simply join your life with mine. Learn my ways and you'll discover that I'm gentle, humble, easy to please. You will find refreshment and rest in me. For all that I require of you will be pleasant and easy to bear **(Matthew 11:28-30 TPT).**

In your day of danger may the Lord answer and deliver you. May the name of the God of Jacob set you safely on high! May supernatural help be sent from his sanctuary. May he support you from Zion's fortress! May he remember every gift you have given him and celebrate every sacrifice of love you have shown him. May God give you every desire of your heart and carry out your every plan as you go to battle. When you succeed, we will celebrate and shout for joy. Flags will fly when victory is yours! Yes, God will answer your prayers and we will praise him! I know God gives me all that I ask for and brings victory to his anointed king. My deliverance cry will be heard in his holy heaven. By his mighty hand miracles will manifest through his saving strength. Some find their strength in their weapons and wisdom, but my miracle deliverance can never be won by men. Our boast is in the Lord our God, who makes us strong and gives us victory! Our enemies will not prevail; they will only collapse and perish in defeat while we will rise up, full of courage. Give victory to our king, O God! The day we call on you, give us your answer! **(Psalm 20:1-9 TPT)**

WALK IN YOUR AUTHORITY AND OVERCOME

Declare: _____'s *identity is not in autism.* _____'s *identity is in Jesus.*

Autism is only a diagnosis and not part of _____'s DNA. _____ has Jesus' DNA.

Let us pause and breathe. Remember, I am speaking to the diagnosis, not your baby. Go back to the previous chapters if you are still struggling with attaching the diagnosis to your child.

I have witnessed for myself and have had the pleasure of ministering to families all around the world how, if they let it, autism can dictate their entire lives. Where they can eat, go to church, when and where to have family outings. Autism has stolen lives. Not for long!

Autism not only attacks an individual. It attacks families, friendships, and communities. It attacks dreams, hope, and peace. It undermines confidence, destinies, and freedom. This is how I know without a doubt that autism is a lie from hell. It causes us to question our future and our children's future. One of my favorite, familiar Bible verses is Jeremiah 29:11. The Message Bible translates it as, *"I know what I'm doing. I have it all planned out—plans to take care of you, not abandon you, plans to give you the future you hope for."* If God has promised to give us a future that we hope for, yet the autism diagnosis leaves you with insecurity and uncertainty for your future, then it cannot be from God.

Autism has already been defeated. It was defeated on the Cross more than two thousand years ago. Together we are going to take authority in our power and render autism powerless and helpless! I know that at this very moment your beautiful baby is most likely screaming or stimming and autism seems to have all the power, but it does not.

We serve a God who has since the beginning of time, proven Himself to be unusual and operates in the unthinkable. I do not know about you, but I refuse to put Him in a box. My human mind can only go so far. It has to make sense of "natural" things. But we serve a supernatural God. I want you to go beyond where your practical, logical mind will take you. When I hear people say, "I am just literal, realistic," I do not know if they realize that their closemindedness keeps God in a box. We literally serve an unrealistic—in our capacity of thinking—God.

I do not want you to ignore autism, I want you to face it head-on. From this moment forward, you are going to tell it where to go. Not to live vicariously through me and Londyn but tap into your own God power. How are you supposed to do this? You rest. Rest in knowing that God cares about you.

I love how the Passion Translation puts Luke 12:6-7:

> *What is the value of your soul to God? Could your worth be defined by an amount of money? God doesn't abandon or*

forget even the small sparrow he has made. How then could he forget or abandon you? What about the seemingly minor issues of your life? Do they matter to God? Of course they do! So you never need to worry, for you are more valuable to God than anything else in this world.

The New King James Version says, *"But the very hairs on your head are all numbered."* So if God cares about hair that sheds, is cut or plucked, why wouldn't He care about what matters to you most. Your child's future and destiny. Your future.

The only way you can tap into your authority is to spend time with the authority giver, Jesus. The One all authority has been given to. The Bible is God's Words, His text message, and social media post for us to be encouraged daily. It is His Living Word that feeds our mind, body, and spirit. We cannot *live* without it. Jesus is the Living Word made flesh.

It is okay to highlight facts of the diagnosis in your posts during Autism Awareness month in April, but I did a self-awareness check. My social media posts that highlight my frustrations and circumstances should never be more than the God who can crush any circumstance and ease my frustrations. My life and social media highlights should reflect God's victory in my life.

Go ahead and participate in events that bring awareness to autism. What an opportunity to build relationships—not to promote religion, but like Jesus, meeting people where they are.

PUT ON YOUR UNIFORM AND TAKE AUTHORITY

In society we have authority figures who wear their uniforms proudly. When they are clothed in their uniforms, there is a unique authority, honor, and respect when we encounter them. In Christ, we all have an indestructible uniform.

> *...the belt of truth tied around your waist and the protection of right living on your chest. On your feet wear the Good News of peace to help you stand strong. And also use the shield of faith with which you can stop all the burning arrows of the Evil One. Accept God's salvation as your helmet, and take the sword of the Spirit, which is the word of God* (Ephesians 6:14-17 NCV).

Our fight is not against people. It is against rulers and darkness of this world (see Ephesians 6:12). We are soldiers for Christ who have been given the authority against and over them. Therefore, make sure that you wear your uniform daily.

God is watching, waiting, and willing to meet all of our needs. You are worthy to receive all that He has for you! I grasped hold of this revelation by not being bound to or a prisoner of autism. I put the God who created me back in control over my life and saw autism as an opportunity, not a crisis. I know by our testimony that God has used our diagnosis to reach the masses. Londyn and I have met and will meet more wonderful people along this journey.

We have reached nations and some wonderful people have been blessed by what I have shared on social media, television, radio, and articles. To get to this point, I had to know that I was not being punished, nor was God punishing my innocent child. I *had* to get here so that I could fully trust Him with her.

As long as the enemy can deceive you into thinking it is your fault that your child has autism, you will not begin to see how God wants you to see them live their full-potential and abundant life.

Another truth that you need to know in order to take authority over autism is that God is not punishing you for your past sins. I love the story in John 9:1-3,32 (NKJV):

> *Now as Jesus passed by, He saw a man who was blind from birth. And His disciples asked Him, saying, 'Rabbi, who sinned, this man or his parents, that he was born blind?' Jesus answered, 'Neither this man nor his parents sinned, but that the works of God should be revealed in him.' ... Since the world began it has been unheard of that anyone opened the eyes of one who was born blind.*

Jesus wanted us to know that even a sinless life did not prevent this man from being blind, but through his journey, the work of God was revealed in him. I am confident that Jesus knows the plans for our lives. I thank God for my life and Londyn's. Through this journey of healing from autism, the works of God are being revealed in us.

OVERCOMERS!

Autism overcomers—everyone affected by autism and are committed to defeating it—God wants His works revealed in your lives too. As long as we believe that we have to take what life gives us, even though Jesus took everything, we will again not see our lives in full potential. I remember dealing with so much guilt and shame because of her diagnosis. All of my casual conversations led to Londyn being diagnosed with autism—as if that was all her life had to offer. Uh uh, nope, autism will not rule our lives!

Oh, and Mom and Dad, stop being so hard on yourselves. You are doing the best that you can do based on the little information that you have. From this moment forward, you are going to have all the information that you need because we are going to the Source to get it. You will no longer work for autism, but autism will work for you. Through overcoming, you will see how God can use any situation, test, and trial for His purpose, His good and perfect will in your life (Romans 12:2).

You are going to take authority over autism. In order to do this, we will begin by getting a full picture and definition of the diagnosis so that we can take authority over it by prayer and confession. Parents often inquire about Londyn's accomplishments. They are always amazed when I explain to them that we indeed had a rough start, and most of them had front-row seats. I made the decision to go to the Source for direction and answers on how to best parent her so that she will live a life full of triumphs and success. What I have learned during our journey is that autism is not any different from any other diagnosis. People are diagnosed with different disorders and diseases and are living functionally while walking out their healing.

Here is how I did it. I applied the Word of God to every situation, trial, and circumstance that we have faced. I am not encouraging you to discontinue any therapy, services, medications, or any intervention that has been either prescribed or suggested by your physicians and providers. As a matter of fact, Londyn continues to receive speech, occupational therapy, and special education services. By utilizing the Word and our wonderful providers, we continue to see great improvement. Londyn is living out her full potential and we see and expect growth. It certainly takes a village. Seek God and He will personalize and build your village with the right people. I will not endorse or speak against any method you are using, just be led by God. I have also been encouraged to alter diet, use supplements, devices, and other interventions.

Think of it this way, how long have you known that the sky is blue? One day years ago, someone told you that it was, you believed the person, and you have never even questioned it. You probably never think about the sky being blue. You just know, and no one can convince you otherwise. That is the faith that I hope you will grasp onto while reading and praying your prayers to the God who is watching, waiting, and willing to answer. Again, Jesus did not forget anything when He took everything on the Cross. As a matter of fact, He stayed there until It. Was. Finished. (See John 19:30.) He wants His best for you!

This will require faith. You will be challenged and will tap into emotions that maybe you are not ready to deal with. As I am writing these words, I realize I still have some sore spots too.

That is why you have to do your uniform check. Continuously fill your spiritual tanks with the things of God. You cannot give what you do not have. Running on fumes will not get you far.

I asked Londyn when she was seven years old during Autism Awareness Month to tell me what autism meant:

April 13, 2015, Facebook post and video:

> From her own mouth! It's AMAZING how she equates autism with doing BIG THINGS! An impromptu video on her own thoughts about her "diagnosis." I love how she gave me an example of "communicating differently." I asked her, "Why" does she have autism because I understand how she comprehends language. She listed all of the songs that she sang in public over the years. #LondynSpeaks #liub #LondynlovesUinblue
>
> Me: Londyn, do you know what autism is?

> Londyn: So you go the capitol, and you get to go to The White House you can sang and say, "Wha, la, la" that's why you go and sing at.
>
> Me: Do you have autism?
>
> Londyn: Yep!
>
> Me: Why do you have autism?
>
> Londyn: Because I sang Take Me to the King and Greatest Love of All and I sing for Aubrey's birthday
>
> Me: Do you know what it means to communicate?
>
> Londyn: Communicate is when if you don't know what to say you just go back to your mom or dad and your brother and your sister and your baby sister.

If Londyn knows that she was diagnosed with autism, but identifies it with singing her favorite songs and singing to friends, then why would I as her mother lessen my outlook of her abilities. You can take authority and overcome autism and not allow it to overcome you.

Despite the evaluations, IQ score, and psychological examinations, she believes having autism is getting to do cool things like sing at the Arkansas State Capitol. I decided that my perception of her and her future would be the same. She does not belong to autism; she belongs to God.

Faith is seeing before seeing. It is so important to see your autism overcomer more than what your eyes can see right at this moment, even if you are literally watching a meltdown while reading this sentence.

Declare this: "_____ belongs to God and not to autism." Words have power and the Bible tells us there is life and death in the power of our tongues and that those who speak with care will be rewarded (Proverbs 18:21).

Remember, our autism overcomers are labeled and spoken over daily by teachers, therapists, doctors, themselves, and by us. It is important that we walk in our authority so that God's confession over us and our children will prevail.

Look to God as your Source and not people. There is a worldly system and then there is the Kingdom of Heaven. I am not going to blame any administration or political party. There are issues that lead to one bottom line—money. There are people making the majority of the decisions that impact the well-being of individuals, yet they do not or cannot relate to their needs. Most of these decisions are made because of a price tag. The only way you can beat the system is overcome it by declaring that it does not control you. I personally do not wait for people to authorize benefits.

I call on the One who daily loads me with benefits (Psalm 68:19 NKJV). I praise God for governmental resources, but people will change their minds to suit themselves. Our God changes not, and His Word is the everlasting truth that endures through all generations. See God as your Source! Not a job, governmental program, insurance. I would rather depend on Him. Keep speaking the Living Word over yourself and your children. Choose today to speak life. In your moments of frustration when words come out that you should not speak, come against those words with the light of the Word. I have to do this daily.

Write down the negative words that you have said about yourself, your family, and your situation in the past few days. Do not hold back and do not be ashamed. Remember, God is not intimidated by your moments of frustration; in fact, He has been waiting on you to talk to Him and not at Him. Pour out your heart.

NOW TAKE AUTHORITY

We must start by detaching ourselves from something that we now know that God did not give us. Remember, autism is only a diagnosis, not DNA. When I introduce people to Londyn, I introduce her as Londyn, autism overcomer.

Put this into practice. Ask the Holy Spirit to help you say, "_____is an autism overcomer." Stand on Job 22:28 (AMP) *"You will also decide and decree a thing, and it will be established for you; and the light [of God's favor] will shine upon your ways."*

Decree and declare: "_____ is an autism overcomer and is walking in their healing!" This will require faith and lots of it. During an impossible meltdown, decree and declare, "_____, you are an autism overcomer. You are healed!"

As you are writing out your own personal prayers and declarations, you are going to start believing that God is for you and your family. He loves you! He wants His best for you! One of my favorite Scriptures that I have held on to during our journey is Matthew 6:11, *"Give us this day our daily bread."* Paraphrased, "We acknowledge You, Lord, as our Provider of all we need each day!" Remember Matthew 6:11 and say this out loud: *"God, You are my Source."*

And when you are worried about insurance denying medication, you say, *"God, I acknowledge YOU as my Provider of all we need each day."*

When lawmakers are cutting federal programs, declare, *"God, I acknowledge YOU as my Provider of all we need each day."*

When the awesome teacher you trust gets a promotion and moves away, *"God, I acknowledge YOU as my Provider of all we need each day."*

Let us not put our BIG GOD in a box that cannot even begin to hold Him. When you know who you are and who God is, you are not worried about your needs being supplied. Declare that *He* is your Source—not a job, insurance, or governmental assistance. I praise God for these resource opportunities, but people change their minds. God never changes (see Numbers 23:19).

> Write this as big as you can: GOD DID NOT GIVE _____ AUTISM! I AM NOT BEING PUNISHED FOR MY PAST SINS. JESUS HAS ALREADY PAID FOR THEM!

Feel free to add anything else that's on your heart right in this very moment.

_____

_____

_____

In this chapter, I will break down the definition of autism and apply the Word of God to each component so that you can take full authority NOW. Every Scripture, prayer, and confession will be specific for each component of the definition. Remember, *the Living Word can and will apply to any thing and any situation in your life.*

FAITH IN ACTION

Play a recording of the Bible. I play it while we are away from home and when we sleep.

Ask yourself this out loud, "Does _____ know he or she has autism? Does my child even know what it is?" Now go and ask the child. Write down the response.

_____

_____

_____

_____

Reshape your words in describing your child. From now on, use "autism overcomer." The Bible says in Proverbs 18:21 (TPT), *"Your words are so powerful that they will kill or give life, and the talkative person will reap the consequences."*

PULL OUT A CHAIR

You must grieve the person you were expecting when your overcomer was born. This may take some time. I want you to stop for a second and do something. Pull out a chair and place it in front of you as if you could see God sitting there. I tell you this, He is there. Tell Him about your day from the time you woke up until this moment. Tell Him every detail and do not hold back on every emotion that you have felt. Remember, God is not offended by your words. Even if you do not want to mention certain things, He already knows. When we open up to God, we are saying that we trust Him to intervene and take care of us.

If you are still struggling, repeat after me, "Jesus HELP!" It is that simple. Now wait for His instructions and get quiet. When you are empty, say, "God, pour into me."

Pull out the chair and reflect, then write what comes from your conversation with God.

_____

_____

_____

_____

HOMEWORK: PROPHETIC ACTIVATION

I want you to prophesy over your children:

1. Get quiet and spend some time in worship and prayer, with or without instrumental soaking music.

2. Take a pen and paper and write or draw what you see, feel, and hear. It may also be a song or poem. Note: It is important that you stay focused on God as you write. Sometimes our human minds cannot comprehend what He reveals. Remember, we walk by faith and not by sight (2 Corinthians 5:7).

3. Sign and date it.

4. Share it with your overcomer and hang it in his or her room. Say something like, "This is what Jesus says about you. This is how much He loves you!"

5. Praise and thank God for what He revealed to you.

6. Refer back to the prophecy to inspire and build your faith.

7. Repeat often. He may even give you words for family and friends. He still speaks; He is just looking for listeners.

8. Connect with a church or small group that teaches prophetic activation and flows in the spiritual gifts. The foundation for all spiritual gifts is love.

SCRIPTURES TO STAND ON

Do not fear [anything], for I am with you; do not be afraid, for I am your God. I will strengthen you, be assured I will help you; I will certainly take hold of you with My right hand [a hand of justice, of power, of factory, of salvation] **(Isaiah 41:10 AMP)**.

Blessed be the Lord, who daily loads us with benefits, the God of our salvation! Selah **(Psalm 68:19 NKJV)**.

Those who live to bless others will have blessings heaped upon them, and the one who pours out his life to pour out blessings will be saturated with favor **(Proverbs 11:25 TPT)**.

Give all your worries to him, because he cares about you **(1 Peter 5:7 NCV)**.

Finally, be strong in the Lord and in his great power. Put on the full armor of God so that you can fight against the devil's evil tricks. Our fight is not against people on earth but against the rulers and authorities and the powers of this world's darkness, against the spiritual powers of evil in the heavenly world. That is why you need to put on God's full armor. Then on the day of evil you will be able to stand strong. And when you have finished the whole fight, you will still be standing. So stand strong, with the belt of truth tied around your waist and the protection of right living on your chest. On your feet wear the Good News of peace to help you stand strong. And also use the shield of faith with which you can stop all the burning arrows of the Evil One. Accept God's salvation as your helmet, and take the sword of the Spirit, which is the word of God **(Ephesians 6:10-17 NCV)**.

If imperfect parents know how to lovingly take care of their children and give them what they need, how much more will the perfect heavenly Father give the Holy Spirit's fullness when his children ask him **(Luke 11:13 TPT)**.

Yes, whoever continues to ask will receive. Whoever continues to look will find. And whoever continues to knock will have the door opened for them **(Matthew 7:8)**.

God is not a human being, and he will not lie. He is not a human, and he does not change his mind. What he says he will do, he does. What he promises, he makes come true **(Numbers 23:19 NCV)**.

LET'S START FROM THE BEGINNING

Londyn was born on Saturday, August 11, 2007, at 7:31 p.m., weighing 7 pounds, 1 ounce and measuring 20½ inches long. I had some postpartum complications that landed me in ICU an extra three days, but her dad would bring her to see me. I remember how her big, beautiful brown eyes would stare into mine as if staring into my soul. She knew I was her mama. She was well attached, and as easy as a baby could be.

My grandma came from Louisiana and lived with us until she was six months old. I loved leaving and returning to find them asleep in the same spot. Life was happening in the most perfect, textbook way. Londyn met all of her early milestones and was very attentive and alert. I remember hearing her babble her ABCs at nine months thinking, *"Wow she's going to be a genius!"*

As a mom, in my mind I began to plan out my daughter's future. Will she be a teacher, nurse, doctor, or lawyer? I saw her with many friends and loud, fun sleepovers. I imagined the many playdates we would go on while the moms talked girl talk. I imagined elaborate birthday themes with countless kids who look forward to our parties. I would put her on waiting lists for the best schools because I knew she would rank high academically. I had her life planned perfectly, as most parents do.

At the age of six months, God sent Granny Irma into our lives. She took care of Londyn until she was three years old. Londyn was being loved by her as her dad and I worked every day, and we did not have to worry about her well-being.

Londyn's first birthday came, and I could see that my niece Kristyn, who is also the same age as Londyn, was talking when Londyn was not. We lived in Memphis, Tennessee, at the time, while my family lived in Little Rock, Arkansas, so I did not have a child to compare her to. In the back of my mind the thought was simply, *She'll catch up. You may not understand what she's saying, but I do.*

At Londyn's 18-month checkup, our pediatrician asked me how many words she spoke, and I could not think of any, wow, not one. She was such a great pediatrician and suggested we get an evaluation. *An evaluation? How do you do that? Is that necessary?* I grew up knowing people who had received speech therapy and they seemed fine. No big deal, right? Dr. Reed sent a referral for services but the diagnostic clinic told me there was a six-month waiting list just to receive a speech evaluation. *A six-month waiting list? Is it that serious?*

I was worried, and I did not have that kind of time. I finally found an early intervention agency that was willing to make a home visit to look her over. That is exactly what they did—"looked her over." The intake worker spent less than thirty minutes with her before telling us Londyn just needed to be around more kids, and if we would go ahead and put her in a day care, she would eventually catch up; affirming my original thoughts.

I remember the intake worker implying that we were making a big deal out of nothing. I had to forgive myself and her, but we will touch on that later. It was the worse advice we could have received from a professional, but I know it was all part of God's plan to transition us to where He needed us to be. For purpose.

My family wasn't convinced, and suggested we move to Little Rock to have better access to more preventative care. It was so scary, but we were at least moving closer to our family. The uncertainty would soon be fixed and I would not be alone, right? Then came the move! The big transition. I remember thinking, *I'm moving back to my hometown. This transition is going to be simple.* There was still doubt. Memphis had been my comfort. I know you can relate to the feeling that comes when that comfort changes. No matter how you prepare yourself to be ready, your heart just is not in it. I quickly learned that although I considered myself very adaptable, I was beginning a journey that would challenge my ability to just "go with the flow."

Reality set in. Expectations would not be met as quickly or at all. In a room full of people who knew and loved me, I was alone. We lived less than two miles away from Kristyn and were around more kids Londyn's age. I was constantly reminded how delayed she actually was. They all seemed so far ahead while Londyn was so far behind. I did not understand why. *I* understood her. *I* could feel her. *I* knew her, but no one else did; and to be honest, there were times when I didn't care. If it was going to be us against the world, then so be it. Praise God for deliverance from that mindset because that is not how He wants us to live.

My baby always measured in the 98 percentile or higher. She had been around bigger kids, and Kristyn seemed to be nearly half her size. When they played together, Londyn would overpower her with strength that she did not understand she had. I always felt myself defending her and honestly it did not seem to help. If my family did not understand what we were going through, how would strangers understand? For the first time my innocent, beautiful, brown-eyed girl was the bully child. She was only three, she didn't understand, and I was quickly shutting down. Helpless. Lost.

School was starting and I was terrified. Londyn was leaving the comfort of Granny Irma and going to a place where there were strangers. Everything was happening so quickly. Because of what I was experiencing at home, would it have negative effects on Londyn at school? Would the teachers not like her and treat her differently because she couldn't talk. The only reason why I had some ease was because I was offered a teaching position at the same school where she would be attending.

I was stressed, and this transition was not helping our marriage. I was wasting away in depression. I saw myself as a failure. Transparent moment: I would look at Londyn and think, *Why can't you just be normal?* I never really cried about it, but the pain consumed my body. I was constantly sick, and I remember a relative saying to me, "Why are you always in the bed?" That is what depression, hopelessness, and helplessness will do. It will take a person who is vibrant and carefree to a dark, dark place.

Above all, I felt so guilty and ashamed for thinking negative thoughts toward my innocent child. I would say many times, "God, Londyn is innocent. She didn't ask to be this way. Why are You punishing her? Why are You punishing me?"

Note: While writing these words, I had to pause and take a deep breath. God is here. I want you to take a moment and write down every thought that is coming to your mind, even if you do not live with autism or if the thought has nothing to do with autism. (Use a separate sheet of paper or write on the lines provided here.)

_____

_____

_____

What if her teacher is mean to her? What if the kids notice and will be mean because they see she is different? With the little strength I had, I asked God that Londyn would at least enjoy school enough to not cry all day. God took the little that I had to offer and answered my prayers.

Her pre-K teacher, Ms. Doris, was an answer to prayer. She was so loving and patient. Londyn had never been around other children before, and she would cry as soon as I dropped her off. God placed Ms. Doris there just for us. Because I also worked at the school, I would sneak off to check in on Londyn. Ms. Doris understood what her needs were. She would sit and hold her all day long until she was used to the new environment. Ms. Doris is a great example of how sometimes you just have to focus on what a child needs at that moment. She would have been well within her rights to call me daily and leave frustrated messages on my phone—but thankfully she was patient and understood Londyn's needs.

Even though God sent her for Londyn, it did not stop the pain and shame that I experienced every day after I dropped her off.

We were at a Christian school, so there was a chapel service every Wednesday. Londyn would have to be taken out because when she saw me, she would scream for me. I was dying inside. "Why, Lord! Why?"

I saw it in her eyes, pleading, *I'm crying for you, mommy, why won't you come and pick me up?* I could still hear her screaming even after she left the room. Talk about a moment of helplessness and shame. *What kind of mother am I?*

Then one day, the crying stopped. She was okay. I felt less guilty.

I pray that what I have said so far has shown you that you are not alone.

TWO IMPORTANT ACTIONS

I am so excited to share with you how Londyn and I became autism overcomers. Before we move forward, there are two important things you have to do.

First: Give your children back to the Lord. This is not the same as having that special dedication service where they wear a poofy dress or bow tie. This is totally surrendering your rights and control to the One who created them. The One who will always know more about them than you ever could. The One who gave His life for them. Give them back to the One who will follow them to places you will never hear about or be able to go. He is their ultimate Protector; and frankly, He is much better at it than we can ever be. Here is what I told the Lord and would like you to declare with me:

> You know what, God, I can't protect _____
> like You can! I don't want to try anymore! I speak Your
> Words over them and I'm leaving them at Your feet. You

are their first love, not me. Forgive me for being in the way when I should be directing them always to You. Help me to show them how to call on You so they will know that when I'm not there, You're always there. You already promised me in Your Word that You are my Refuge and Fortress (Psalm 91), so I give _____ back to you now.

Second: Forgive! If you are like me, forgive yourself if you did not get help immediately when you noticed delays. Forgive family members for their lack of patience, understanding, and help. They did not know how to. Yes, forgive that lady at the grocery store last week that shot you that "You're a horrible parent!" look. You are not a horrible parent. Forgive your spouse for not responding the way you think he or she should have. Londyn's dad and I are now divorced, but I am glad that I received the revelation that men and women are just going to respond differently. I praise God that he and I are on a journey of co-parenting God's way.

Now, I encourage you to write down everything that you have been holding in your heart in anger against anyone, even yourself. After you have written it all, give it to the Lord and *forgive!* Get more paper if you need to. Write it all down and you may find yourself adding to the list in the days to come. Do not hold back. Take the weight off of you; Jesus always intended to carry it anyway.

> *Casting all of your cares [all your anxieties, all your worries, and all your concerns, once and for all] on Him, for He cares about you [with deepest affectionate and watches over you very carefully]* (1 Peter 5:7 AMP).

I forgive

I want to forgive

I will do it with you: "I forgive the agency in Memphis, Tennessee, who regarded my concerns as 'You're a new mom and this is common.'"

Truth moment: Answer each of the following sections and give this burden to Jesus.

- I want you to deal with the hurt of being dismissed by a loved one or friend because of your concerns.

- I want you to deal with the hurt and anger that you have because a professional dismissed your concerns. Most likely you now approach clinicians and educators on the defense and I completely understand that you cannot help it. There is nothing more annoying than someone trying to convince you that they know more than you do regarding your children. Some of you cannot wait to run into them so that you can show them that they were wrong! Your child can walk. Your child can talk. And your child is functioning.

- I want you to also deal with the regret and shame because you "missed it."

I will be honest with you. My mom and sister were sharing their stories of coworkers and friends whose situation reminded them of Londyn. I never disagreed, but I was numb. I literally did not know how to move forward. What were the next steps? Who was I supposed to call? What kind of doctor did she need? I was clueless at what to do and also, there was not a lot of forthcoming information that would have helped me along the way.

Later as my knowledge increased, I always felt like there was a secret society of services that only a "select" few were offered. I could not understand or grasp as to why Londyn was improving, yet some of my other friends were having the hardest time. Autism showed me a world that I had never seen before. It does not matter the color or socioeconomic status.

I want to remind you of this, God gave that baby to you. If you are reading this and have any concerns that have not been addressed, call your child's pediatrician in the morning. I have practiced this important tip. If they will not listen, find someone who will.

NOW TAKE AUTHORITY

Go to a mirror. Look into the mirror at yourself and I want you to say your name, "_____, I forgive you." This is a start; add whatever else is on your heart.

FAITH IN ACTION

Like I did, release the "us against the world" mentality. God wants you in relationship.

How much time do you spend with your closest relationship—spouse, best friend, relative? Set a timer and spend that amount of time talking to God. Remember to always take pen and paper with you. Try and increase over time. Before long you will be spending hours and cannot get enough.

If you do not know how to pray, start here:

> *In this manner, therefore, pray: Our Father in heaven, hallowed be Your name. Your kingdom come. Your will be done*

on earth as it is in heaven. Give us this day our daily bread. And forgive us our debts, as we forgive our debtors. And do not lead us into temptation, but deliver us from the evil one. For Yours is the kingdom and the power and the glory forever. Amen" (Matthew 6:9-13 NKJV).

Or simply acknowledge you need help by starting with, "Jesus, help me!" He can and will help you.

HOMEWORK

Pull out your chair: I want your conversation with God to reflect the beginning of your child's journey on earth. Start where I did: birthdate, weight, etc. Talk to God about your feelings of your child's beginning until this very moment. Write your reflections.

SCRIPTURES TO STAND ON

For we have the living Word of God, which is full of energy, and it pierces more sharply than a two-edged sword. It will even penetrate to the very core of our being where soul and spirit, bone and marrow meet! It interprets and reveals the true thoughts and secret motives of our hearts **(Hebrews 4:12 TPT)**.

Do not fret or worry. Instead of worrying, pray. Let petitions and praises shape your worries into prayers, letting God know your concerns… **(Philippians 4:6-7 MSG)**.

The Lord kept every promise that he made to the Israelites. There were no promises that he failed to keep. Every promise came true **(Joshua 21:45)**.

For every word God speaks is sure and every promise pure. His truth is tested, found to be flawless, and ever faithful. It's as pure as silver refined seven times in a crucible of clay **(Psalm 12:6 TPT)**.

For if you embrace the truth, it will release more freedom into your lives **(John 8:32 TPT)**.

Our faith guarantees us permanent access into this marvelous kindness that has given us a perfect relationship with God. What incredible joy bursts forth within us as we keep on celebrating our hope of experiencing God's glory! **(Romans 5:2 TPT)**

But if you live in life-union with me and if my words live powerfully within you—then you can ask whatever you desire and it will be done **(John 15:7 TPT)**.

ADIOS DIAGNOSE

So we are convinced that every detail of our lives is continually woven together to fit into God's perfect plan of bringing good into our lives, for we are his lovers who have been called to fulfill his designed purpose.

—Romans 8:28 TPT

Diagnose Adios: A phrase used to characterize the nature of a clinician's actions after diagnosing autism.

THE A WORD

Now we're getting somewhere. Arkansas did have better access to services and Londyn almost immediately received speech therapy. With the advice from our early intervention team, we moved her to a developmental pre-school. Because we were persistent in our journey to learn more about Londyn's needs, we were soon referred for a comprehensive evaluation.

Londyn was diagnosed with autism in January 2012 at the Dennis Developmental Center. I remember someone telling me, "Hey, just so you know, April is Autism Awareness Month; wear blue and get all of your family and friends to do it too." Finally! We're getting somewhere. I immediately thought, *I can do that. I'm going to shine a light.*

April 2, 2012

World Autism Awareness Day…less than three months after Londyn's diagnosis.

My Facebook post: *Our "1"—she will ALWAYS be #1 to us! Autism is a lifelong neurobiological disorder which currently affects 1 in 88 people in the US.*

April is Autism Awareness month and this post would be the first time that I shared with the "world" Londyn's diagnosis. I remember getting so many private messages on social media, phone calls, and text messages as family and friends got the news. Support came from everywhere. To be honest with you, at the time I wanted the "fuss," but I did not know what all the fuss was about. Did I miss something? She was still Londyn to me. Still my normal baby.

Later on, numerous friends would offer for me and Londyn to come and live with them for support. Was it that serious? For the first time, as I am typing these words, I realize that I was in denial. I had the assurance that God was in control, but I was going to ignore autism without facing it head-on.

When I wrote the Facebook post, I had no idea what I was getting myself into. I was a mom who was a go-getter and problem solver. My mom taught me to have my tantrum, but to do it quickly and get ready to walk toward a solution. Autism was no different. I got this. Londyn has it. So what!

I was in denial.

I saw where other parents were posting daily statistics and sharing articles. "Cool, I can do that too." It was like a reassuring notion that we could somehow get through this journey as long as we fight the good fight by wearing blue, getting our family and friends to do it too, and posting on Facebook. HA!

I could check these things off of my list of how an effective autism parent gets down to business. I would soon learn that this is the world's way and not the way that God would have us respond to a diagnosis. I was beginning to wear "Autism Mom" like it was a badge of honor. It was more important for me to have this identity, but I was forgetting that I already had an identity. I was created in the image of God.

This journey was going to take more than wearing blue and posting on social media. After the official diagnosis, although I already knew what the outcome would be, I remember thinking about how Londyn would have this *label*. It was so official. So permanent. As Londyn's mom I felt *my control* over her life was slipping away. There were a lot of people telling me things about her that I did not know, understand, or like. Even though I had accepted the diagnosis, *Londyn was my baby!* How could I have missed that something was wrong? After all, I carried her for 39 weeks and 6 days.

I did what I was supposed to do. I prayed for her daily while she was in my womb. I went to all of my appointments. I followed the prenatal guidelines. I even gave up sushi, well, except that one time, but it was my birthday and my doctor said I could. Most of all, after she was born, I looked into her beautiful, bright eyes every single day and saw a happy, healthy baby. How could I have missed that she was delayed? She was going to now need several doctors, therapists, and special schools. Why did everything just have to be *special?*

You have probably heard of the Kubler-Ross model for the stages of grief: denial, anger, bargaining, depression, and acceptance.

When I walked out of "the dark room" where she was officially diagnosed, I was ready. I told myself, *"This is what it is and you got this."* I literally was functioning as a person in the stage of acceptance. All smiles. No cares of this world. In reality, I was oblivious to what that diagnosis meant. I was oblivious to my feelings. Worst of all, I was beginning to rely more on research and science than the One who created her.

God created science; if you want to know the true Source of information, you have to go to Him. It is just that simple. You would not go to a car sales associate if you are having problems with your eyesight. You would go to an eye doctor.

Many times we do not take the time to ask God. A problem occurs and we immediately go into autopilot frustration mode. We react through social media posts and conversations, among other ways. We do not settle ourselves to ask the very Person who sees all and knows all. I love the way The Passion Translation puts it:

> *Don't be pulled in different directions or worried about a thing. Be saturated in prayer throughout each day, offering your faith-filled requests before God with overflowing gratitude. Tell him every detail of your life, then God's wonderful peace that transcends human understanding, will make the answers known to you through Jesus Christ* (Philippians 4:6-7).

I decided that I was not going to be a slave to autism. I will bring awareness by shining a light, THE LIGHT...Jesus.

I want to give you some tools to help you with this. In "The Best Road Trip Ever" chapter, I talked about gathering your support system who will go on the journey with you. One of your journey members must be a person you view as a spiritual mentor. This person is a great sounding board, but will always point you back to Jesus. Who is your person? _____

AN ADVOCATE IS BORN

In December 2012, I had a follow-up appointment with Dr. Lopez, Londyn's developmental pediatrician. I never felt intimidated by her. We had her undivided attention during our visit. She never blew us off, she listened. We compromised. More importantly, she asked about our home life. She was concerned about the whole child. The focus was not as much on the diagnosis, but coping with it. This is so important. I strongly recommend that you find a developmental pediatrician who cares not only about the diagnosis, but about your child's whole self and the total well-being of the family.

In addition to being an awesome doctor for Londyn, she offered me a gift that I will always cherish. Before we ended our appointment, she told us she loved how Londyn and I were so connected and how I responded to her. She asked me, "What do you do?"

I replied, "For the past year I have been a stay-at-home mom to focus on Londyn, but I really want to mentor parents. Be a shoulder that they can cry on during this process."

She said, "Let's do it! I'm going out of town, but I will email you as soon as I get back."

I honestly thought, *She's too busy and probably will not get back to me.* Two weeks later, she emailed, and before I knew it, I was one of her parent mentors. All it took was someone to see something in me and take the time to get to know us.

In my bed, December 2012, PAAK was birthed. PAAK—Parent Advocates for Awesome Kids. Our mission is to inform, mentor, and support families through prevention and intervention services by empowering families to promote the best interest of each individual child.

We wanted to create a support system that would help families with the evaluation process and emphasize the critical importance of early intervention to families who have concerns related to their child's development, including autism spectrum disorder. If families and childcare providers had concerns about how a child was learning, behaving, and interacting with others, we offered support.

PAAK's continuing goal is to encourage and help families seek assistance in order to promote the best interests of each individual child. We have provided information through small group sessions, webinars, and academic support for medical students across the country. We have also received high honors by being the Arkansas Children's Hospital *2016 Ambassadors for Autism*. Our prayer is that our journey will reach parents who need *hope—Jesus*.

We take joy in providing one-on-one family support to help families navigate the system, such as help with completing paperwork, preparing for an evaluation, and assisting those who "get stuck" on a specific step. We have reached families as far away as Germany.

LEADING A GROUP

When I started PAAK, many people talked about how they really wished they could start their own organization. I even had several inquire about joining forces. I do not recommend doing *anything* without the guidance of the Holy Spirit. It does not matter if family or friends think it is a great idea. When He gives you the go, He will have already prepared you for what is to come.

Carrying others' problems on your shoulders is dangerous. We were not meant to—that is His job. We can minister, encourage, empower, lead, and support, but not to the detriment of our own health, sanity, and well-being. So make sure you are ready before committing to lead a group and definitely know that God has graced you for it.

If someone you know is thriving in what you believe God has graced you for, do not get discouraged. Here is a revelation that the Holy Spirit gave me years ago when I knew He called me for a specific anointing:

> The tennis shoe has different name brands, but they all serve the same purpose. Nike has a vision. Adidas has a vision. Skechers has a vision. A Nike tennis shoe is not a Skechers tennis shoe. Same purpose, different visions. God's purpose for you is unique!

Isaiah 43:19 (NLT) says, *"For I am about to do something new. See, I have already begun! Do you not see it? I will make a pathway through the wilderness. I will create rivers in the dry wasteland."*

I think the important words of this Scripture that we often overlook are "dry wasteland" and "wilderness." God is showing us there will be uncomfortable seasons in our lives. He wants us to be excited about the new He is about to do in our lives, but He also wants us to know that He is the Pathway and the River for what is to come with the new. The wilderness and dry wastelands are opportunities for growth.

When God first revealed His new thing that He was about to do in my life, I was so excited. I finally knew my purpose, my calling, and I was sure that the people close to me would be just as excited, especially because I was always excited about what God was doing in their lives. I quickly learned that I would need the Pathway and River really soon. Not everyone can ride along with you to your next destination. I had the audacity to follow God's will by risking the loss of some things, to gain everything.

God told me that our journey would be used to bring souls to Him. Because of my audacity to follow God's will, He has blessed me with the opportunity to be a testimony to His goodness. And guess what? He wants to use you too.

My friend, believe what God has said to you! When you spend time with Him, He will give you dreams beyond what you can imagine. Trust the bold, confident, and spiritually aware person that He has made you to be. Say "Adios!" to the diagnose.

Now Take Authority

I want you to have the experiences that I have had—because each has brought Londyn and I closer to God and true joy and peace.

Are you satisfied with your healthcare providers? Ask the Holy Spirit to lead you to the right village.

Faith in Action

I dare you to ask God for something that would seem impossible in your own thinking. Who would have thought that I could be a stay-at-home mom even after my divorce—but I asked Him, and I am.

What are you afraid to ask for?

God cares so much about our feelings and what is "insignificant." Even when He told us not to worry, He still cares about that.

Confess this out loud when you arrive to work: "Today is my last day working at this job. I am standing in faith that I will be a stay-at-home_____." I dare you to ask what seems unrealistic in your human thinking.

If you do not desire to stay at home, but would like a less stressful job, write out your job description. Be very specific and even include the salary.

In August 2018, I felt led back to the workplace, so I wrote out my job description and by the end of September, I had the job that I wrote about…exactly. I strongly encourage you to trust the only Source, God.

Remember, if you decide to start a support group, always approach people's different viewpoints in love. I have learned to not try and change their minds; rather, I introduce love, honor, and wisdom.

HOMEWORK

We talked about the stages of grief: denial, anger, bargaining, depression, and acceptance. Where are you? Be honest.

_____

_____

_____

Pull out a chair and talk to God about it. Ask Him to tell you where you are. Sometimes we have an inaccurate idea of how we really feel. Take your pen and paper.

_____

_____

_____

Make post-it notes of Scriptures or anything you learn while reading. Have your child write in his or her journal as well. If they cannot express in words, let them draw pictures, use Legos, or any form of art. I believe that we have the freedom to express our love for God in our own way. He is our Creator, and it is obvious that He loves to create beauty…like you! He wants to awaken our creativity by speaking to us through it.

SCRIPTURES TO STAND ON

> *Yes, it is God who is working in you. He helps you want to do what pleases him, and he gives you the power to do it* **(Philippians 2:13)**.

> *The earth and everything on it belong to the Lord. The world and all its people belong to him* **(Psalm 24:1)**.

> *This is what the Lord God says: "Look, I will wave my hand to the nations. I will raise my flag for everyone to see. Then they will bring your children to you. They will carry your children on their shoulders, and they will hold them in their arms. Kings will be their teachers. The daughters of kings will care for them. The kings and their daughters will bow down to you. They will kiss the dirt at your feet. Then you will know that I am the Lord, and anyone who trusts in me will not be disappointed"* **(Isaiah 49:22-23)**.

> *God can do anything, you know—far more than you could ever imagine or guess or request in your wildest dreams! He does it not by pushing us around but by working within us, his Spirit deeply and gently within us* **(Ephesians 3:20 MSG)**.

> *You have given miraculous signs to those who love you. As we follow you we fly the flag of truth, and all who love the truth will rally to it. Pause in his presence. Come to your beloved ones and gently draw us out. For Lord, you save*

those whom you love. Come with your might and strength! **(Psalm 60:4-5 TPT)**

I can do all things [which He has called me to do] through Him who strengthens and empowers me [to fulfill His purpose—I am self-sufficient in Christ's sufficiency...] **(Philippians 4:13 AMP)**.

May we never forget that the Lord works wonders for every one of his devoted lovers. And this is how I know that he will answer my every prayer **(Psalm 4:3 TPT)**.

OVERCOME SPEECH

April 3, 2013, Facebook post

> Who would have known that "1" day this sweet face would be told that she would always be "different." We always knew she would make her mark, but we never imagined her mark would create a lifelong masterpiece! We are the luckiest, blessed people on Earth to have birthed such a gift. Londyn, I am honored to call you my baby and to be your mommy! The Bible says that we are to be a peculiar people (1 Peter 2:9). Well, Londyn you are a hearer and do-er of His word! Autism may be in our vocabulary, but it will NEVER DEFINE YOU!!

In order for us to reclaim our identity in Jesus, we have to first reject the identity of autism. In 2018, according to the Centers for Disease Control and Prevention (CDC) their definition for autism spectrum disorder is:

> Autism spectrum disorder (ASD) is a developmental disability that can cause significant social, communication, and behavioral challenges. There is often nothing about how people with ASD look that sets them apart from

other people, but people with ASD may communicate, interact, behave, and learn in ways that are different from most other people. The learning, thinking, and problem-solving abilities of people with ASD can range from gifted to severely challenged. Some people with ASD need a lot of help in their daily lives; others need less.

Londyn and I said NO to every word in autism's identity. By doing this, we were able to overcome it. When you receive any identity, it defines you. If you are "okay" with the autism diagnosis and do not see a need to take authority over it, this CDC definition not only defines you, but will describe your daily life.

When you take on the identity of Jesus, *He* defines you!

Speech is where it all begins. Waiting to hear your child's first words is a parent's dream. We look forward to this great milestone. We even make a playful competition out of it. "What will she say first, Ma-ma or Da-da?" Words give us a glimpse of their personality. Children can tell us how they are feeling and what they need.

When reality sets in and we realize they are not talking like other kids their age, we become numb and helpless. We cope by accepting "their way of communicating." For me, I was comfortable in speaking *Lon-dish*.

It was not until my mom said, "You know she can learn how to talk" that I realized the possibility of intervention. The thought never crossed my mind. I honestly did not know there was a problem. I understood her, that was all that mattered. This gave me a glimpse outside of our world and my own understanding.

It is so important that we ask the Holy Spirit to help us with this. He will open our minds and hearts to receive. My way of thinking was not healthy for her growth, and I am glad I had someone to point that out. In my Caregivers chapter, I give insight on how you can support a parent who needs encouragement.

EARLY INTERVENTION

Let me guess! You were told that your cousin's mama's baby sister who is twice removed on your grandma's side did not talk until she was almost seven. She is *fine* now and you are overreacting because you had or may have concerns. I am sure you have an example of this same conversation with your friend and/or loved one about your own child.

In the previous chapters, we talked about forgiveness. Please refer back to them if this statement triggers emotions.

Communication is the foundation for everything we do. Through pictures, words spoken and unspoken, movement, art, and music, we are constantly communicating—and in autism, this is the Achilles' heel.

Because Londyn is overcoming language and speech delays, I find myself learning and receiving my very own version of speech therapy. I realize that I am not the great communicator that I thought I was. I am from the south and we love to use slang and idioms. I remember saying to Londyn, "Baby, hit the light for me." Can you imagine the look on her face? It was pure confusion? The only thing that she could relate to hitting was a ball. The "light" was way above her head. I am sure that although she wanted to obey, it was just impossible.

My favorite example, which I know you can relate to, is when she would talk in hergibberish and if I could not translate quickly, it would set her off. The funny, not-so-funny part about it all was

I pretended to understand what she was saying and she could see right through me.

I had to model what an effective communicator looked like and that did not always involve actual speaking. I had to become her best teacher, rather than focus on her developmental delays. Spending time in prayer, worship, and reading God's Word will help you with this. He is *the* Best Teacher.

During Londyn's early preverbal stages it became very clear to me that she not only communicated through speaking, but touch, emotions, facial expressions, and body language. If either of these were "off," it would easily trigger a meltdown, and fast. This journey of autism had me unnecessarily stressed, and I did not have a choice but to continue this journey with her. Londyn was so sensitive to my every move; I was so conscious, maybe even overly conscious, of how I acted in every moment. Every moment mattered. What if my actions led her to over-process a thought that would cycle through her mind endlessly?

At first this was hard. Knowing that the raising of my eyebrow would signal to her that something was not okay was tough. To be honest, it was like walking on eggshells. Let me take it a step further—the spirit of fear was creeping in and setting root into our lives.

"So what am I supposed to do about it, Angeletta?" You cannot afford to dismiss this as "This is our reality; we are used to this." You have to take authority over it, otherwise that fear will overcome your life. Your decisions will be controlled by fear. Your outlook on your child's destiny will be filtered through fear. You will not believe that you can *Take Authority Over Autism* because of fear.

Just like the thoughts in your head are a broken record repeating your worst fears over and over again, you are going to have to replace them with the Word of God. At the end of this chapter are Scriptures to stand on against fear. Confess them and put them on repeat through Bible apps and videos.

"MOMMY, I THINK YOU HAVE AUTISM LIKE ME."

The Holy Spirit taught me how to communicate with Londyn about her diagnosis and not treat it as the plague or a secret. Whenever she struggles, we talk about it. I ask her how she is feeling physically and emotionally. Londyn and I had the best conversation about her echolalia. She said, "Mama I can't stop talking to myself."

I asked her what is happening when she talks to herself. She replied, "I have a lot of thoughts in my mind, and I am anxious."

So we prayed together and asked the Holy Spirit to calm her thoughts. We confessed that her mind was just like His and He would take away all anxiety. I told her she did not have to feel badly about it, just trust in the Holy Spirit and ask Him to help her.

Londyn said, "Mom, I think you have autism because you act just like me."

With a puzzled look of uncertainty, I said, "Okay, honey." Minutes later I said, "Angels, go before us and prosper our ways!"

She overheard me praying out loud and said, "See, you have echolalia too! You speak your thoughts out loud."

The moral of the story is our overcomers are watching us. Their minds are big sponges that soak up everything they see or hear. They look to us for validation before they know who Jesus is. When we receive our identity in Jesus and not in a label, our overcomers will do the same.

The story of Moses is one of my favorites in the Bible. Even Moses, who was chosen to deliver God's people out of slavery in Exodus 4:10, did not believe he was fit because of his speech and communication delay. I love God's response to him, *"Is it not I, the Lord? Now go! I will be with you as you speak, and I will instruct you in what to say"* (Exodus 4:11-12 NLT). We have to trust that God will teach our children how and what to say. If He can use Moses to deliver a nation, He will use your autism overcomer.

Here are tools that I used:

1. I asked the Holy Spirit to help me process words and communicate clearly and effectively. This is not limited to those with a diagnosis. My quiet time with Him allowed me to do a self-check, so that I would be able to model what effective communication looked like.

2. I became best friends with her Speech Pathologists (SLP). Whatever Londyn learned during therapy was reinforced at home. I loved how her SLP communicated with Londyn's teachers to make sure that everyone was in one accord for her academic success.

3. It takes a village! If she was going to be with family or friends, they followed our pattern.

4. I patiently corrected her by replacing her words with proper grammar. Remember, we have to model our expectations.

5. I did not "dumb down" any of my communication to her. I spoke to her at the age-appropriate level

even during her preverbal stage. By doing this, I was putting my faith into action.

6. I confessed God's Word over her speech, language, and communication. I recognized that our help comes from Him. Psalm 124:8 (TPT) says, *"For the same God who made everything, our Creator and our mighty maker, he himself is our helper and defender!"*

7. I reminded myself that all of these tools would take time and consistency. Celebrate the "small things."

8. I gave myself a pass, which means I accepted and received God's grace when I was too tired to attempt all these tools.

I am just going to be honest—some days, I just did not do any of these tools. The list goes on and on and I found out quickly that worrying and stressing would not get me anywhere. I hate when I am misunderstood by anyone. And kids on the spectrum are no different; they really struggle with this too. I am glad that we have the Holy Spirit. If we will allow Him, He will lead our lives to possibilities beyond what we can ask or think.

I went to the Word. This is what I confess over Londyn:

Londyn has good advice and common sense to offer. Londyn has understanding and power. With Londyn's help, kings rule, and governors make good laws. With Londyn's help, leaders govern, and important officials make good decisions (see Proverbs 8:14-16).

One of my favorite things to share is, "When Londyn couldn't talk, I prayed and prayed that she would. My prayers were answered and I can't get her to stop talking!" She is so matter of fact and literal. There were definitely times when I would wait, cringing, for what Londyn was going to say. She spoke her mind. She knew what she wanted, well beyond what I could have taught her or could have modeled for her. I love that about her. She gave a firm yes and no; and when her mind was made up, there was no turning back. I had to go in prayer and ask God how to navigate her personality and strong determination.

I had to remind myself daily that I am not alone. As I mentioned earlier, replacing fear with His Word and meditating on that over and over again has made me believe it. It is true when you hear something over and over again, you will believe it.

Christ lives in us and we can overcome anything! To date, Londyn has publicly shared her story in front of congregations, school leaders, politicians, and during autism events. At age seven, she sang the National Anthem at the 2014 Autism Walk in front of 2,500 people. How is this possible? By receiving God's identity and believing that He wants us healed.

Now Take Authority

Ephesians 3:20 (TPT) says:

> *Never doubt God's mighty power to work in you and accomplish all this. He will achieve infinitely more than your greatest request, your most unbelievable dream, and exceed your wildest imagination! He will outdo them all, for his miraculous power constantly energizes you.*

Declare: I praise You, God, for _____'s language and communication skills, and I speak in my full authority that his or her speech and language abilities are lined up according to your Word. God, with Your power working in me, You can do much, much more than anything I can ask or think. It says so in Your Word in Ephesians 3:20. God, I give You my anything that I can ask or think—and because You have already promised that You honor Your Word (Psalm 138:2), I know it's already done. Thank You!

Now I want you to write your own prayer, your (anything that you can ask or think) concerning your child or children's communication, speech, and language. Don't hold back. Ask your God, who hears and answers (1 John 5:14-15).

From this point forward, this is the pattern that you are to follow when writing your prayers.

John 14:13-14 (TPT) tells us:

For I will do whatever you ask me to do when you ask me in my name. And that is how the Son will show what the Father is really like and bring glory to him. Ask me anything in my name, and I will do it for you!

Start or end your conversation below with "In Jesus' name."

FAITH IN ACTION

Preverbal: "They follow because they are familiar with his voice. They won't follow a stranger's voice…" (John 10:4-5 MSG). We do not use the term "nonverbal," we use "preverbal," because we always stand on faith that they will soon speak. At this moment they may not speak words, but they have a voice.

What do you imagine their first conversation with you will be like? Faith is action, it is seeing before seeing. *"For we walk by faith, not by sight"* (2 Corinthians 5:7 NKJV). Write that imagined conversation:

Role-play: Londyn and I role-play before introducing her to a new situation. This allows her the opportunity to adapt to change, to prepare, and have time to process. Note there will be times when you will have to repeat a scenario several times before they understand it.

The echolalia signaled me to pray: When I noticed she was doing it more, I knew to pray for her. The echolalia is her way of finding her place of peace. When she went to that place, I told her to repeat after me: "Jesus, I receive Your peace. Thank You for never leaving me." I also whispered a Scripture over her (Isaiah 26:3). When she heard the Scripture, it replaced her repeats of cartoons or conversations that she'd heard. Can you imagine the magnitude of power when our overcomers are constantly repeating His Word! Also, ask your child's teacher(s) if they notice any changes in his or her speech and behavior. This will keep you on your prayer alert.

Confess over your kids: "_____, you are just like Jesus." Take time and enjoy your spiritual food. Please do not rush while reading Scriptures together.

Educate: Take time to educate people without being on the defense. I had to learn that I am not going to always be with Londyn in every situation. I have to give her the tools to get through it. I have had to educate local businesses and their employees on how she processes information. There were several incidents that left her in tears, but we did not leave the scenario until Londyn understood what had happen. The employees also learned a valuable lesson. This will train her to adapt to change and allow her time to process. This will also open the conversation on compromising, something we all need to learn.

When was the last time your pastors prayed for you? James 5:14 (TPT) says, *"Are there any sick among you? Then ask the elders of the church to come and pray over the sick and anoint them with oil in the name of our Lord."*

PRAYER

Father, I thank You for my life and the lives of my family and friends. I thank You for giving me Your identity. Now that I know that I do not belong to autism, I will take authority over it. I will no longer focus on setbacks—rather, I will focus on victory. I give it all to You. I will not allow anger to rule in my life. I thank You for changing my mindsets and giving me new ones. I thank You for giving me _____.

I struggle with adapting to change and need time to prepare and process. Show me how to be my child's teacher, but to also come to You, the Best Teacher.

I speak Your peace over our minds, bodies, and spirits. Our thoughts are Your thoughts, our ways are Your ways. We do not have any deficits, especially concerning our attention. We operate in pure focus!

I make a lifestyle commitment to pray fervently to You concerning _____. I will enjoy Your spiritual food daily. Your Word is life. Show me how to be patient and enjoy Your peace because You have promised it in Isaiah 40:31.

SCRIPTURES TO STAND ON

Trust the Lord with all your heart, and don't depend on your own understanding **(Proverbs 3:5 NCV).**

For God will never give you the spirit of fear, but the Holy Spirit who gives you mighty power, love, and self-control **(2 Timothy 1:7 TPT).**

Now Christ lives his life in you! And even though your body may be dead because of the effects of sin, his life-giving

Spirit imparts life to you because you are fully accepted by God. Yes, God raised Jesus to life! And since God's Spirit of Resurrection lives in you, he will also raise your dying body to life by the same Spirit that breathes life into you! **(Romans 8:10-11 TPT)**

Take this most seriously: A yes on earth is yes in heaven; a no on earth is no in heaven. What you say to one another is eternal. I mean this. When two of you get together on anything at all on earth and make a prayer of it, my Father in heaven goes into action. And when two or three of you are together because of me, you can be sure that I'll be there **(Matthew 18:18-20 MSG)**.

Love never brings fear, for fear is always related to punishment. But love's perfection drives the fear of punishment far from our hearts. Whoever walks constantly afraid of punishment has not reached love's perfection **(1 John 4:18 TPT)**.

You keep every promise you've ever made to me! Since your love for me is constant and endless, I ask you, Lord, to finish every good thing that you've begun in me! **(Psalm 138:8 TPT)**

Jesus became wiser and grew physically. People liked him, and he pleased God **(Luke 2:52 NCV)**.

OVERCOME EMOTIONS

He gives strength to the weary and to him who has no might He increases power.

—Isaiah 40:29 AMP

"Echolalia" is defined as the unsolicited repetition of vocalizations made by another person.

Truth moment: While I am typing this chapter, Londyn, now ten, is drying tears from a brief misunderstanding—a mini meltdown. I call it a misunderstanding because it is not quite a meltdown, yet it is beyond crying. Londyn has been picking at a sore that cannot heal. I snapped at her, "Leave it alone!" The Holy Spirit quickly said, "You've picked at sores that you should have left alone." OUCH! How many times have I picked at a sore because I could not help it, yet He did not snap at me? I am so glad that He never condemns, only corrects. She sobbed because I hurt her feelings, followed by lots of echolalia: *"I can't help it, it itches. It's okay, Londyn. I can't help it, it itches."*

I honestly don't know what is worse—not knowing what Londyn was trying to "say" or not knowing how she felt. There were moments when I knew that I could not fool her anymore. She knew that I was lost. I felt so powerless. Her emotions kept me lost in translation. There were moments when I thought everything was okay, but her echolalia would prove otherwise. I could barely figure myself out to know what I wanted, and now I had to "guess" about what she needed.

I have many conversations in my head where I am yelling at the top of my lungs, "I don't know what to do! What do you want from me!" And my favorite, "We're not going to be #supermom today, Cookie. You tried boo, you tried." I soon realized that until I released that energy from me and trusted the Lord to guide me on what to do and what to say to support Londyn, that negative energy would only transfer to my actions toward her. Because that is exactly what energy does.

My negative energy would cause her to be more off balance. If I was unsure, so was she. I am so glad that I made it a priority to talk to God about it.

There were definitely days when I waved the white flag. Does this sound familiar? You are all cried out, prayed out, and tired of fighting autism. Being consistent is not fun! It seemed like I could help navigate people through their experiences, yet I struggled and still felt alone. Then I thought, *I honestly didn't think I could be the perfect parent for a typical child, so why did you decide to give me a special child, God? You must really see something in me that I cannot. God, You promised to never leave. Where are You?*

I realized that I was operating on a check-off system.

- Prayed for Londyn (insert check mark)
- Prayed for her therapist/teachers (check mark)
- Told autism where it could go (3 checks)

Overcome Emotions

God wanted me to rest in knowing I could trust Him. He wanted me to realize that our relationship was so important to Him. It was not about the perfectly rehearsed prayers or strategically written confessions. It was just the two of us—the three of us.

Holy Spirit, Londyn, and me working together would be the ammunition to fight against the meltdown (cue the Rocky theme song). In the early days I honestly did not fully understand what was going on when Londyn was having one. I am ashamed at how I reacted to her. I was so angry: *Why can't she just calm down? Why can't she understand me? Why does everything have to be such a big deal?*

Going to the One who knows her best without us trying to figure it out and guess, is the only solution. He showed me I was not just dealing with a meltdown. I was dealing with a peace thief. Her melting down and my walking her through it was stealing our peace.

I began to show Londyn that during a meltdown that she was to walk out First Peter 5:7 (AMP):

> *...casting all your cares [all your anxieties, all your worries, and all your concerns, once and for all] on Him, for He cares about you [with deepest affection, and watches over you very carefully].*

I dealt with meltdowns and autism like I would deal with anything that is not of God. I had to take authority over it. I told it, "You aren't going to ruin our day. Our vacations. My baby was not going to cry. She was going to have peace, because peace is a promise that Jesus keeps. It is her birthright."

I asked the Holy Spirit to show me how to see ahead. Most importantly, He showed me how to help her command her own peace. I asked Him for wisdom in my choices for Londyn. Most of

101

her frustrations were because she wanted to be understood. I asked Him for that as well.

Because of this diagnosis, you have probably experienced the following emotions: sadness, anger, fear, anxiety, disgust, depression, shame, envy, guilt, resentment, jealousy, frustration, pride, and rage. Are you tired of being tired? Overcoming will take effort and sacrifice. You will have to do things that require more time—but trust me, His Way has everlasting benefits. I spent a lot of time getting myself together so I would have something to give. If I was empty, how could I give anything to Londyn?

Maintain a Full Spiritual Tank

How full is your spiritual tank? If it is not a priority to you, there will be repercussions. Our tanks must be full and our children must have a full tank.

Because I am not sure what Londyn has been exposed to when she is not around me, the first thing I do when I see her is make Jesus the focus. I do this by music, prayer, or just talking about Him. In the Environments chapter, I go in-depth on how to do this. Tank filling is so beautiful, we can *never* be too full of what God has for us. His grace, peace, joy, love, and more.

If you are empty, ask Him to fill you up. Ask Him to show you how to stay full. I know exactly what you are thinking because I have thought it myself, *I don't have the time. By the time I get my child to go to sleep, I'm exhausted.* Have you ever asked God to manage your time—or do you have your schedule all planned out? This is a very important aspect to consider in overcoming.

Make sure that you make deposits into your spiritual tank. It will never overflow. God's love, peace, and joy will overtake those negative emotions when they begin to rise up. You cannot do it on your own. I cannot do it on my own. Even today, I am making sure that my spiritual tank is full.

Still you may say, "Angeletta, when will I have time?" Our bodies rest, but our spirit never sleeps. When I am so consumed by negative emotions, I fall asleep to worship music, Scriptures, messages by my pastors or other pastors I admire. Before you know it, God's wholeness and "everything coming together for your good" will settle you down. It is wonderful what happens when Christ displaces worry at the center of your life.

I found that the strongest power comes from the direct Source. We can watch our favorite TV show, drown ourselves in work or our favorite hobby, but true peace can only be found in Him. I speak peace over my autism overcomer and her emotions: "God, You can go places I cannot go. You can understand what I cannot understand. It makes me feel helpless and powerless as a parent to not know. I receive Your peace. Give me wisdom, knowledge, and understanding. I give You every hurt, pain, and emotion."

You can ask God to put you in tune with your child's emotions. I have heard Londyn's audible voice call my name even though I was far away from her. When I said out loud, "Yes, Londyn." Others around me said, "Girl, Londyn is in a separate part of this building; it is impossible to hear her." I immediately went to where she was and sure enough, she had called my name and needed me.

The following are some tips regarding emotions—yours and your child's:

1. Monitor their spiritual tanks. If you know their day has been fueled by chaos, play light worship music while they eat, sleep, or bathe.

2. Monitor your spiritual tank. Play soft music. Remember, they are hypersensitive to your emotions and easily feed off of how you're feeling.

3. Do not try and fake your feelings. Londyn knew when something was off. I took the opportunity to settle my spirit—calm my nerves—before interacting with her. Remember, you absolutely cannot give what you do not have.

4. Pray these words over your and your child's emotions: *"Whenever my busy thoughts were out of control, the soothing comfort of your presence calmed me down and overwhelmed me with delight"* (Psalm 94:19 TPT).

5. Ask the Holy Spirit when to approach your child about feelings. I know that when they come home from school upset, your instinct is to dive in with a million questions. (I'm guilty.) If you are anxious, it will cause their anxiety to elevate.

6. While you are waiting to approach them, pray! Ask the Holy Spirit to minister to them as well as minister to you. After He calms your thoughts, you will be able to hear and speak clearly to your overcomer without being overwhelmed with your emotions.

Autism attacks our emotions. I cannot even imagine the depths that it attacks our child's emotions, but it most go. The blood of Jesus can and will go where we cannot.

Now Take Authority

Fill in the blanks: _____ belongs to You, God, and not to autism. I stand on Your Word that _____ is the head, and not the tail; I will be above only and not beneath as it says in Your Word in Deuteronomy 28:13. _____ is made in Your image, so because You do not have autism, _____ is victorious over autism.

> Declare: *"For whatever is born of God overcomes the world. And this is the victory that has overcome the world—our faith"* (1 John 5:4 NKJV).

Faith in Action

Here is an example of a confession I wrote in 2013:

> ### *Jesus, Angeletta, and Londyn Freedom 2013*
>
> I thank You, Lord, that according to Your Word in John 14:12-14 (NKJV): *"Most assuredly, I say to you, he who believes in Me, the works that I do he will do also; and greater works than these he will do, because I go to My Father. And whatever you ask in My name, that I will do, that the Father may be glorified in the Son. If you ask anything in My name, I will do it."*
>
> I thank You that You are the Man who will not lie. Your Word says, *"God is not a man; he will not lie. God is not a human being; his decisions will not change. If he says he will do something, then he will do it. If he makes a promise, then he will do what he promised"* (Numbers 23:19).

Because Londyn and I believe and do Your works, we know that whatever we confess on this page, it will come to pass.

The blood of Jesus covers me and Londyn all the days of our lives. Favor, goodness, and mercy surround us daily! **Everything we touch is blessed.** Everyone we come in contact with will be blessed and will be a blessing! We are money, favor, goodness, mercy, peace, joy, wisdom, and love magnets! And we only attract these things!

We will LIVE and not die and declare the works of YOU! **Everything we touch is blessed!** We have sound minds and are not easily distracted! Angels encamp around us because we fear the Lord. Jesus is number one in our lives. We have a personal relationship with Him! We are blessed and highly favored with increase on my mind, in our hearts and in manifestation.

Now write your own confession:

_____
_____
_____
_____
_____
_____

The following are some prayers I have prayed:

Father, I break the chain of autism over _____ (kids, family, self). It will not attack their emotions. I speak Your Word over them—They will have cheerful hearts, their spirits will not be crushed, and their bones will not be dry. I declare that You are our strength every morning and You have turned our mourning into dancing.

We receive Your peace. We come to You with our heavy hearts, and we receive Your rest. Worry, you must go! I have peace. I will not spin like a top. I give it all to the Prince of Peace. I cannot do it by myself.

Because it is released to You, I will no longer worry about juggling relationships, being a super parent, failing at relationships, or feeling helpless when Your are solutions around me. Father, show me how to command Your peace and their peace. _____ wants to be understood; show me how. Reassure them that they have You. Even when I am not with them, they will always have You.

Lord, give _____ dreams about You. Show him/her the future. Lord, there are going to be things that I will never be able to explain. Even with the help of the best textbooks, it is hard to understand their emotions. I can't even understand my own. But You understand them. You created him/her. I put him/her in your hands. Holy Spirit, I want to be just like You. Teach me how to be a helper, advocate, standby, comforter, intercessor, counselor, and strengthener. In Jesus' name, amen.

Write some of your prayers:

HOMEWORK

Print off peace Scriptures for your child or children to read on their own. Even if they do not understand what they are reading, God's Word is feeding their spirits. If the child cannot read, play the Bible app while he or she is playing. Trust me, God has a way; we just have to receive His grace.

Close your eyes and get quiet. Now utter words of worship. For example: "Thank You, Lord." "I worship You," or sing a song to Him. Sometimes, I felt mute and did not have the words. As long as I took the first step of getting quiet, He did the rest.

Let it go: I remember feeling I *had* to address the elephant named autism. There were awkward moments when I blurted out, "She has autism, so I'm warning you not to be alarmed." Rather, give it to Jesus and say, "Jesus, I give it all to You."

Now list all of the things that you need to give up. I will help you start: Wanting to be in control. (Ha!) Your turn.

You must take authority over terror, anxiety, panic, and torments. You do this through warfare. Speak firmly (out loud) and tell the enemy to leave you and your family alone. Or my favorite, "Mind your own business! You didn't create me or die for my sins. You don't get a say-so in my life!" Praise and worship confuses the enemy.

SCRIPTURES TO STAND ON

Lord, be kind to us. We have waited for your help. Give us strength every morning. Save us when we are in trouble **(Isaiah 33:2)**.

He stooped down to lift me out of danger from the desolate pit I was in, out of the muddy mess I had fallen into. Now he's lifted me up into a firm, secure place and steadied me while I walk along his ascending path **(Psalm 40:2 TPT)**.

You will teach me how to live a holy life. Being with you will fill me with joy; at your right hand I will find pleasure forever **(Psalm 16:11 NCV)**.

So above all, guard the affections of your heart, for they affect all that you are. Pay attention to the welfare of your innermost being, for from there flows the wellspring of life **(Proverbs 4:23 TPT)**.

…make "peace" your life motto… **(Psalm 34:14 TPT)**.

OVERCOME SOCIALIZATION AND RELATIONSHIPS

Say, "God, I know that I am Your favorite daughter/son."

In "The Best Road Trip Ever" chapter, my goal was to show you the importance of not wearing isolation as a badge of honor. We just cannot have an "us against the world" mentality. We need people. God created us that way. There is nothing honorable about being alone. I want you to refuse isolation. Jesus gave us this great example when He walked on earth. He was always in a social setting. He only went alone to pray, be reenergized, and get instructions from His Father.

The Bible is very clear in Ecclesiastes 4:9-10:

Two people are better than one. When two people work together, they get more work done. If one person falls, the other person can reach out to help. But those who are alone when they fall have no one to help them.

I can honestly say that I struggled with isolation. I am "used" to doing things on my own. I did not like to ask for help or accept it. I just went on, pretending that autism didn't bother me. The reality is, there was rejection there. We do not want to be rejected, and we definitely do not want this for our kids. So, we tell ourselves that we are good. We are in a routine and do not have the time to socialize. I cannot speak for you, but I made excuses. I remember being so nervous introducing Londyn to new kids. I did not want her around other children. Truth moment: I did not want to hate your child!

Londyn was always the tallest in a group of kids. She was so strong, not angrily aggressive, but her strength could be overpowering. When she played an innocent game of tag, her hits were not equal to theirs. When she thought she was giving a playful hit, the other kid got the most damage.

I hate that she was misunderstood; and honestly, I was dealing with my own hurt and it had nothing to do with people or Londyn. The rules were not fair, so I "protected her." I tucked her away. Furthermore, it was best that I did not get upset with a child who misunderstood Londyn—this was very inappropriate of me and I have repented for this. I told myself she would rather be at home in her own world than meet friends. Yes, three-year-old Londyn could make logical decisions for herself. I thought that this was our life: isolated, secluded, and forgotten. Of course, I deceived myself into thinking I was protecting her. But my protection was going to eventually hinder her from experiencing possibilities and opportunities.

There was a time when I did not think Londyn would be able to participate in activities. We heard about this awesome dance class led by "Miss Andree," which is what Londyn called her. It was just for kids with special needs and we had to try it. I was terrified. *What if they look at her funny? What if she overpowered a smaller kid and the child got hurt?* We stepped out on faith and went. I remember the first time she met her favorite buddy, Riley, in 2011. It is a memory that will forever be in my heart. They were meant to be lifelong friends.

When we got to the class, Londyn walked in and ran to Riley. It was a divine connection. An unlikely lifelong friendship because I made a choice to trust God and come out of isolation. You know what? Londyn is still running to Riley. This is why it is so important for you to make time for social activities, especially the ones designed just for kids with special needs.

Let us also be realistic. Children learn by what they see. The more I isolate, the more she will not be motivated to make friends. There are times when Londyn prefers her "me time" as she calls it. I have told her the importance of being like Jesus and showing yourself friendly. Me time is okay, but it should never outnumber the time that can be spent with wonderful friends. When she wants to get out and socialize in her own way, I have always allowed it. You may have *tried*, but I urge you to model it more.

TAKE A MOMENT

You cannot allow autism to dictate your lives. We cannot allow it to force us to stay at home, avoid relationships for fear of judgment, or stay in a world where no one is allowed to enter. What is your heart saying in this moment?

Pray this prayer: "Lord, just like You had unlikely friendships when You walked on this earth, please send us friends. Your divine connections. We are not looking for friends based on the autism association. We want who You send to us. Open our minds and hearts to receive them."

In a society where unfortunately bullying and isolation is so common on school grounds, I knew that I had to remain in prayer. I prayed for Londyn to have great friends who understood her. I wanted them to help her grow, and I also wanted her to help them grow. I wanted to raise a godly example; but in order to do so, I had to go to God for the answers on how to make this possible.

I began to confess that not only would Londyn have wise friends, but she would be wise as well.

There are going to be growing pains as your overcomer meets knew friends and strives to be socially accepted. There are going to be moments when you cannot be offended. I am not saying that you should keep any hurt to yourself and bottle it all up. I had to put myself in the shoes of the kids who were meeting Londyn for the first time. What would I have thought or said about a child who "talked funny, or talked to herself"? Once I was honest with myself about how I might react, I had to forgive the precious children who would soon meet Londyn.

Most importantly, Londyn was learning to be a good friend. They were going to meet Londyn, and most of them have not met a girl like her or have heard of autism. Although they may have a cousin or knew someone with autism, they still responded with their childlike reactions. I once heard Londyn being referred to as "autism Londyn" by a friend. It was a knife in my heart. She was in a group with another child named Londyn, so that is how the kids referred to my Londyn so they would not get them mixed up. It is moments like these that remind me about the innocent heart of a child. Children are trainable; and although that was an eye-opening moment for me, I had to keep it moving and not dwell on it.

Does your child have any friends? What are their names?

_____

_____

_____

Be honest with yourself about how you really feel. Do you wish that their friends were more typical or more advanced to set an example for them? I had to learn to accept God's provision for Londyn over my preference.

This also became a topic of discussion when it was time to decide if Londyn should be mainstreamed into the general education population or in a self-contained classroom. I had to switch gears on what it may look like versus God's perfect will. I would not have it any other way. Londyn has taught me to be a better communicator, to be aware of my surroundings, and to have patience.

Here are some helpful tips:

1. Always set aside alone time, just you and the Holy Spirit. Bring paper and pen to write down what He says to you.
2. Connect with a local support group.

3. Connect with a church that has a special-needs ministry.

4. When there are organized outings for special needs families, go! This will allow practice for you and your family, for when you want to go to places that you would not have dreamed of going before, because of behavior and embarrassment.

5. Join your local Autism Awareness Organization and sign up for the annual Autism Walk. Again, this is a great way to connect with other families for support.

6. Practice: I took Londyn to a movie where we were the only ones in the theater before going into a busy movie theater with lots of people. Sensory playdates tested her reaction to being in public.

7. Ask God to highlight a person who can be your spiritual support mentor. I thank God for mine.

8. Ask your local businesses to partner with you and host sensory playdates. This will create a space for families who really want to come out of isolation. Since 2016, I have hosted #StrikeOutAutism, which hosts 175 participants on average. Pray first and be led by God.

I want you to be free from the fear and the rejection. Show yourself friendly and allow His love to pour out of you. I promise it will attract lots of good people you need in your life.

Remember it is a journey. If you get hurt, it is okay. We have to remember Ephesians 6:12-13 (TPT):

Your hand-to-hand combat is not with human beings, but with the highest principalities and authorities operating in rebellion under the heavenly realms. For they are a powerful class of demon-gods and evil spirits that hold this dark world in bondage. Because of this, you must wear all the armor that God provides so you're protected as you confront the slanderer, for you are destined for all things and will rise victorious.

I know that is hard because we see a very real person in front of us doing the hurt. A very real person saying nasty things. A very real school official saying something about your child while you overheard them talking. Jesus wants us to see people the way He sees them. Doing it His way always leads to victory. Knowing this gave me comfort while navigating through social cues. Supporting Londyn through understanding others has been like learning a new language.

There really isn't a cookie-cutter way to approach this because every human being is different. Social expression is almost as unique as a thumbprint. I remind myself that this part of the journey takes time and patience. Londyn's heart has been broken because she wanted to be someone's friend, but she did not understand their social cues. The only solution—take it to the Holy Spirit. He cares about our broken hearts (Psalm 147:3).

Here is a confession. Fill in the blanks with your child's name.

_____will walk with the wise and grow in wisdom. Jesus, increase _____in wisdom, stature, and favor with God and people (see Luke 2:52). God, give _____ wisdom and exceedingly great understanding and largeness of heart like the sand on the seashore (see 1 Kings 4:29-30).

I want Londyn to have a heart for God's people. One of the most important things that we can ever ask God for is discernment. Pray that your overcomer will have a double portion of discernment. This will give them spiritual insight on how to understand people.

Besides communicating, I think the social well-being of our overcomers is right at the top of our priorities. What mommy and daddy would not want friends for their kids? We want them to be wanted, invited to parties and playdates. God has always provided Londyn with friends. Her social calendar is fuller than mine. She participates in school, after-school, and church activities. She has auditioned and won major parts in plays. She enjoys volleyball, cheer, dance, piano, and violin. She is no longer hidden. She is my sidekick.

NOW TAKE AUTHORITY

God, I thank You that _____ is full of Your love, joy, peace, patience, kindness, goodness, faithfulness, gentleness, and self-control (Galatians 5:22-23). *I thank You that You are lining up the right friends and advocates at school: the playground, classroom, and cafeteria. I pray for the friend or friends, that they will continue to have patience and show love and kindness toward _____.*
I thank You that _____ is an example of You and will grow through friendships while helping others to grow. I thank You that _____ has good advice and common sense to offer. _____ has understanding and power. _____ helps kings rule and governors

make good laws. With their help, leaders govern and important officials make good decisions.

CONFESSION, DECLARATION, PRAYER

Father, I break the chain of autism from _____ _____ (name kids, family, self). It will not attack us socially. We will have lifelong friendships. Our children are not to be hidden because of this diagnosis— You want their lights to shine brightly. You want them out of isolation and to have great friends. The friends that You send to them. Godly friends. We speak your words over_____. We know that it is good for brothers and sisters to dwell in unity. Lord, You care if we have friends. You had friends. And we are all made in Your image. Thank You for Your grace and mercy in our lives.

FAITH IN ACTION

Every year at Londyn's birthday parties, I would always invite at least twenty-five children. We wanted fellow overcomers to know they are wanted.

If you see a struggling parent, offer support. That first day at I CAN!, I met a nice mom named Sherrie. Her sweet, simple words changed my total outlook. Londyn would be okay with Riley while I enjoyed the opportunity to meet other awesome moms.

Ask God for a very special friend. Londyn's special friend is her sister-cousin, Kristyn. Kristyn has been able to reach Londyn when I couldn't. God graced her with a special portion of love and patience just for Londyn.

Praise God for the little things and keep a journal. Write down the dates of answered prayers. This will remind you that He does hear and answer.

Remember, it's a journey.

SCRIPTURES TO STAND ON

If you want to grow in wisdom, spend time with the wise. Walk with the wicked and you'll eventually become just like them **(Proverbs 13:20 TPT).**

How truly wonderful and delightful to see brothers and sisters living together in sweet unity! **(Psalm 133:1 TPT)**

I am passionately in love with God because he listens to me. He hears my prayers and answers them. As long as I live I'll keep praying to him, for he stoops down to listen to my heart's cry **(Psalm 116:1-2 TPT).**

As one piece of iron sharpens another, so friends keep each other sharp **(Proverbs 27:17).**

Since we have this confidence, we can also have great boldness before him, for if we present any request agreeable to his will, he will hear us. And if we know that he hears us in whatever we ask, we also know that we have obtained the requests we ask of him **(1 John 5:14-15 TPT).**

You draw near to those who call out to you, listening closely, especially when their hearts are true. Every one of your godly lovers receives even more than what they ask for. For you hear what their hearts really long for and you bring them your saving strength **(Psalm 145:18-19 TPT).**

There is no greater love than to lay down one's life for one's friends **(John 15:13 NLT).**

There are "friends" who destroy each other, but a real friend sticks closer than a brother **(Proverbs 18:24 NLT).**

Walk with the wise and become wise, associate with fools and get in trouble **(Proverbs 13:20 NLT).**

Overcome Behavior

Jesus said, "I am the true vine, and my Father is the gardener. He cuts off every branch of mine that does not produce fruit. He also trims every branch that produces fruit to prepare it to produce even more. You have already been prepared to produce more fruit by the teaching I have given you. Stay joined to me and I will stay joined to you. No branch can produce fruit alone. It must stay connected to the vine. It is the same with you. You cannot produce fruit alone. You must stay joined to me. I am the vine, and you are the branches. If you stay joined to me, and I to you, you will produce plenty of fruit. But separated from me you won't be able to do anything."

—John 15:1-5

The beginning of each chapter has started with a declaration or Scripture passage. I want you to realize that even when you think they aren't, your children are always watching you. You are their first teacher. How are we going to train our children to tap into their authority and to know who they are in Christ if we do not do it and believe it ourselves?

Model this: "Jesus, I have Your character. _____ has Your character too."

This area is where I have struggled most on our journey. Our overcomers are judged based on their actions well before they are heard or given the opportunity to share what is so awesome about them. I have witnessed the judgmental faces, mostly from adults, and I became very sensitive about it. I was the parent who before someone even had a chance to *see* Londyn, I would blurt out, "SHE HAS AUTISM!" There were times when I was waiting for someone to say something. I had a fight built up in me and it wanted to be unleashed on anyone even *looking* at my baby strangely.

In this moment I know your mind has taken you to a place where there are hurtful memories.

I want you to take a piece of paper and take a moment to reflect. Write down a moment when you and your overcomer were judged by a look or grumble.

When you are finished, say, "Jesus, I give this to You, and I forgive that person." If you know the person's name, speak it and release that hurt. Now ball up the paper and slam dunk it into the trash! The Holy Spirit wants you to do this as a sign that you are letting go. If the memories still come, and they will, quickly say, "Lord, I forgive." Pull out a chair and release it to Him.

Strangers are not the only ones lacking knowledge and understanding. Sometimes it will be the ones who love you the most. You most likely have asked yourself, *Why can't they understand that there are certain behaviors associated with the autism diagnosis?*

I used to cringe when I was asked about Londyn's stimming, loud humming, and facial expressions. "What is Londyn saying?" Really? You still don't get it? But they weren't alone in their constant questions. I even thought to myself, *How many times is she going to repeat that same line from her favorite cartoon?* Here is a revelation that the Holy Spirit gave me: These behaviors will always be connected to the identity of the autism diagnosis.

The more I took on the identity of autism, I can always expect the behaviors to get stronger and rule in her life. Until I disassociated her with that identity, I could only expect them to continue. I do not excuse her behavior; I take authority over it. She is a mimicker, so naturally I put her in an environment where I did not mind her replicating the behaviors. When she is rude, I tell her she is rude. I give her the definition, then ask her if she that is how she wanted to treat people? Of course, it takes time for her to process what I am saying, but I stand on Proverbs 22:6 (TPT).

> *Dedicate your children to God and point them in the way that they should go, and the values they've learned from you will be with them for life.*

I had to train her by showing her the best Model—Jesus. I wanted her behavioral actions to line up with His. I want her identity in Jesus to rule in her life. I wanted us to live by John 15:1-5, cited at the beginning of this chapter.

The Holy Spirit has shown me ways to help Londyn during her journey to healing. He told me to speak the fruits of His Spirit over her: love, joy, peace, patience, kindness, goodness, faithfulness, gentleness, and self-control. With preparation, wisdom, knowledge, and understanding we are overcoming in this area—and you will too.

The Holy Spirit taught me how to replace each behavior with a fruit of His Spirit. Rather than trying to "change" her, I introduced a fruit that can only come from the Holy Spirit. He will do the changing.

"THE TALK"

Puberty for us started early. I first thought, *Lord, whyyyyyyyy?! Not only is she overcoming day-to-day struggles, but now she has to deal with this?* It was a "Now what?" moment. I stopped and said wait a minute—this is a God-created, natural time in her life. I need to go to Him for answers. Have you ever told God something as if it were new to Him? Like He's never had "the talk" before.

January 14, 2017, will forever be remembered as the day our school community came together fast. I must have walked in the school with a "What's wrong look." I was greeted by staff who immediately went into noooooooooo mode! We literally had an unofficial IEP in the hallway. Everyone was on board and news quickly spread about Londyn's new venture.

Her school nurse said that it would be alright for her to come to the health room to take care of her needs. We alerted all of her teachers and we survived! So do not allow what is natural and from God to be bound by fear of the unknown. Ask God for help. While supporting and empowering parents, I have had many talks about puberty and self-stimulation. Ask the Holy Spirit to lead and guide you. I am fully aware that because of the diagnosis, Londyn requires grace in certain areas, but that is it. I allowed grace to step in. When I am weak, He is strong.

I want to remind you that I am not suggesting that you should stop any practice that has been advised by any professional. If you are using anything and it is working, then keep going. I only urge you to make sure that God is part of your decision making. Besides,

He is going to know what is best for us. He is the only constant. I love hearing breakthroughs from families after they have tried traditional and even alternative medicines and intervention. It is important for us to realize that what may work for your child may not be as effective in Londyn or anyone else's. Jesus is the only remedy that fits all.

THE PIECE TO THE PUZZLE

While spending time with the Holy Spirit, He gave me a revelation about the puzzle pieces. I have observed Londyn when she was really in that *place*. Her echolalia was so intense and all I could hear was a lot of the gibberish. He told me she is going to a place of safety. She does this when she has been stimulated or when she is hurt or sad. If she does not know how to communicate it, she goes *there*.

I prayed this simple prayer to the Holy Spirit, "Show me how to take her to You, so that when she goes to that *place*, she is going to a place where You are. Where she can focus on You and You can deposit into her. Where You will give her understanding of what has happened."

We can pray this! We can show them how to worship. We can help them process after a long gibberish session. I have put this into practice. I ask her what she was thinking? How is she feeling? I told her next time she feels that way, just say, "Jesus, please help me," and then trust that He has it from there. I asked her what happens when the echolalia increased. I meet her at her understanding, and then we ask Jesus to heal it so that the piece is back in the right place. He wants them to tap more into Him and get them out of their heads.

Because I want her to be successful, I cannot make excuses for her. She will say, "But Mom, I'm trying." And I'll say, "I know you are, my sweet girl. You have to put the tools into practice. I know you can! I have seen your genius in action! Look to Jesus when you need help. Wherever you go, He is there. If you go to the tallest mountain and to the lowest depths, He is there."

Then I pray, "Lord, I want her to remain present and focused, but wherever her mind takes her, You are there because Your Word promises it."

Make this Scripture personal by saying, "Jesus, increase _____ in wisdom, in broad and full understanding, and in stature *and* years, and in favor with God and others (Luke 2:52)."

Their behavior is dictated by the environment they are in. In the chapter on Environments, I talk about how the slightest change affected Londyn's reactions. During meltdowns, our first instinct is to react with panic, fear, embarrassment. Rather, command God's peace to come over us.

STEPS WE TOOK

We planned ahead: We always educated Londyn's teachers about what was unique to her. When she does not want to face an obstacle, she will change the subject and hum.

We knew the triggers: I know, sometimes you can feel like you see a new trigger every day, but for the most part, be mindful. The Holy Spirit will help you see what needs to be seen.

We did things she liked: It is easy for them to drift into their own world. I taught Londyn to ask the Holy Spirit for direction. I also told her to confess: "I have a sound mind."

We educated others: Take the time to educate others without being on the defense. There were some things she could not help. I was going to have to be patient while also checking my behavior and responses to her behavior.

I know that it is difficult to determine if some of the behaviors are related to autism or to them just being kids. Remember, we were never told that we had to go through life guessing or trying to figure things out on our own. We have Someone patiently waiting to meet our needs, whatever they may be.

The Holy Spirit showed me how to "check the engine light." When your check-engine light comes on, what is the first thing you do? You may already be thinking, *Mine stays on.* For some parents, this is true even for their kids. They never really seem to be idle; they are always in motion.

What is your child's check-engine light? Hook them to Him and He will do a diagnostic check. I know Londyn's—it's when the stimming and echolalia gets really loud. Then I know it is time to pray. The Holy Spirit will help you, too, just ask.

Be frustrated with the autism diagnosis—not your child. Command authority over the diagnosis and rebuke deficits, recognizing that they are the thieves in your lives. I had a heart-to-heart with Londyn about her echolalia. I am aware that it is very habit forming and attached to the autism diagnosis. I lovingly shared with her God's heart for her to be whole. Echolalia has been a hinderance to her ability to focus. Rather than be frustrated with her, I recognized her journey and how she is learning to command authority over her own life. When her echolalia is intense, she says: *"I operate in complete focus. Echolalia GO! Deficits GO! I have the mind of Christ!"*

Time management: This was my responsibility, not Londyn's. When I looked at myself, I was making excuses and blaming it on autism. God will manage your life, if you let Him. There will be sacrifices. I did not do a lot of what people expected me to do as a single woman because my priority was Londyn. God was showing me that it was beyond that. I needed to honor my call by making my parental responsibilities the priority. He expects me to train her in the way she should go until He releases me.

I saw parenting as the *good work* mentioned in Philippians 1:6. I needed to be ready: my prayer life, my soaking time, and my worship time. I saw that when I was ready and equipped, so was Londyn. Yes, making excuses is so comfortable. I know you have been trying and you are tired. I had to wake up and choose not to want to live like this.

I used the Word; I was tired of autism dictating my life. I have had people look at her and wonder why her behavior is not like most kids on the spectrum. My answer to that is, "It could have been, but I took authority over her behavior." There are videos of her in her younger years that clearly show a difference. Back then, she *looked* like she has autism. Trust in God, and it will work out for your good. Your child will look just like Jesus.

My question and challenge to you: Have you tried God? Did you really give your child's diagnosis to Him, or did you give only half, maybe just 10 percent? Did you try and could not wait on Him? Take some time and try Him. Just like you would wait for a new prescription to get in your system, allow the Great Physician to prescribe His life-changing Word. You *will* get results.

NOW TAKE AUTHORITY

Pray: _____ has the mind of Christ (1 Corinthians 2:16). I call out everything that is not like You and say it is destroyed by Your blood! Lord, I thank You for time management. I know that there are sacrifices, but obedience to You is where I want to be.

FAITH IN ACTION

Remember, you are not going to always be where your overcomer is in every situation. Therefore, give your child the tools to get through different scenarios. Practice with family or friends so that they will be prepared. This will also help with social cues. We have had many teachable moments, especially in businesses. Some of these left her in tears. When she was ready to talk, I took her back to the establishment so she could have closure. We had discussions with the cashiers until Londyn understood and had processed what took place. It was also a teachable moment for the cashiers and will prepare them for interaction with more overcomers.

If you equip them, they will know what to do in times of trouble. Train them to call on Jesus, because there will be times when they may not be able to call on you for answers. He is always waiting on our call. He gave this promise in Isaiah 65:24: *"I will answer them before they call for help. I will help them before they finish asking."*

Play a recording of the Bible while they sleep.

DECREE AND DECLARE

I decree and declare that according to Galatians 5:22-23, _____ has Jesus' divine love.

_____ has joy *that overflows,*

_____ has peace *that subdues,*

_____ has patience *that endures,*

_____ has kindness *in action,*

_____ has a life *full of virtue,*

_____ has faith *that prevails,*

_____ has gentleness *of heart,* and

_____ has strength *of spirit.*

These fruits are limitless in _____'s life.

Before your child goes to bed, ask the Holy Spirit to give _____ a glimpse of the future. Ask Him to guide your overcomer and go deep into the depths of their minds, covering all the places that you could never reach.

Throughout this journey, God wants you to understand that there will be moments when His instructions for you may be to remain still, quiet, and calm. He will do the fighting for you (Exodus 14:14).

SCRIPTURES TO STAND ON

Behold, I'm standing at the door, knocking. If your heart is open to hear my voice and you open the door within, I will come in to you and feast with you, and you will feast with me (**Revelation 3:20 TPT**).

If you withhold correction and punishment from your children, you demonstrate a lack of true love. So prove your love and be prompt to punish them (**Proverbs 13:24 TPT**).

Out of my deep anguish and pain I prayed, and God, you helped me as a father. You came to my rescue and broke open the way into a beautiful and broad place (**Psalm 118:5 TPT.**

Make God the utmost delight and pleasure of your life, and he will provide for you what you desire the most. Give God the right to direct your life, and as you trust him along the way you'll find he pulled it off perfectly! (**Psalm 37:4-5 TPT**)

Listen to my testimony: I cried to God in my distress and he answered me. He freed me from all my fears! Gaze upon him, join your life with his, and joy will come. Your faces will glisten with glory. You'll never wear that shame-face again (**Psalm 34:4-5 TPT**).

So I tell you to believe that you have received the things you ask for in prayer, and God will give them to you (**Mark 11:24 (NCV**).

Whenever my busy thoughts were out of control, the soothing comfort of your presence calmed me down and overwhelmed me with delight (**Psalm 94:19 TPT**).

OVERCOME LEARNING

Common sense and success belong to me. Insight and strength are mine. Because of me, kings reign, and rulers make just decrees. Rulers lead with my help, and nobles make righteous judgments.

—Proverbs 8:14-16 NLT

The following is a confession that I wrote in 2011. I began praying and confessing these words two years prior to Londyn entering kindergarten at Roberts.

> Londyn will be enrolled in a school today that she will love and enjoy going to. Where she can grow and help others to grow. Her school will be surrounded by God-fearing people who are Holy Spirit filled and who do not operate unless they consult the Holy Spirit first. She will excel academically. She will improve her speech, language development, motor skills, and anything that is lacking in her body today!!

I think it is important that we realize that we should always be prepared as parents. I knew that the transition to kindergarten would be major, so I did not wait to begin praying and confessing the night before. I began to stand on His promises two years before it was to come to pass. Can God give us instantaneous results? Yes, and I am a witness. There are, however, benefits to "starting early." The more I confessed this prayer, when the time came, no one could convince me that God was not going to do above and beyond the words on the paper, because I had already built my faith because of it.

I may not have had all of the knowledge that I needed after she was diagnosed, but I knew how to stand on His Word, make my confessions known, and pray. I did not know much about what autism and learning looked like. I was not exactly sure what her future would hold. In the spring of 2011, it was very clear that she needed to go to a *different* school. *But where? How different? Where would we even begin to look?* I had no one to ask or who was in this similar situation.

After spending time in prayer, I did what most would do, I searched the Internet. We began touring different schools and nothing seemed to fit. I am sure the developmental preschools were very knowledgeable and prepared. They had all the bells and whistles, but nothing fit. We would look, then send my mother for a second opinion. I strongly advise you to gather your road trip crew together when deciding on a placement. Plan to go at separate times, and make sure it is also at different times of the day so you can get a complete picture.

Just when we were going to decide on a school, I found a school that did not have much public information written about it. I thought it couldn't hurt to explore. I was not really sold on our other choice; so, why not?

JEHOVAH JIREH—THE LORD WILL PROVIDE

North Hills was exactly what we needed. When we walked into the building, we felt the family atmosphere. Everyone knew our names and without a doubt, Londyn's success was top priority.

Parent: If we do not get an understanding that we do not have the capacity to protect like God, we will drive ourselves crazy.

When she was younger, dropping Londyn off for school was a daily struggle. As a matter of fact. I hung around and peeped into the classroom until I could see that she was okay.

As always, Jehovah Jireh provided exactly what she needed. She transitioned very well at North Hills and received plenty of hugs and kisses when she needed them. It was also time for Londyn to grow and meet expectations. As a parent, I had to be okay with that. I had to let go of the control and "protection."

Our two years there were wonderful, but it was time for the big move. The move that most parents dread. We were faced with three options: public, private, or home school. We immediately sought out private because we believed that she would most likely thrive in a smaller setting.

Here is a perfect example of stopping to pray before believing you know what is best without consulting the One who holds their futures. We toured many types of schools before deciding to go the public route. *We* thought the best possible placement was North Little Rock. Londyn had been a student in that area and she was thriving. Because we had such a wonderful experience there, it was only natural that we go to a school in that area. We started our quest to find somewhere to live.

First, we asked several people about the schools in the area. Of course, just like any other public school, we heard about the elite schools and how hard it was to get accepted. We were told the best thing to do is find somewhere to live in that school's zone. We began putting in applications for housing to live there, but we kept getting denied, which was not normal for us. Our focus was in the wrong place. We were leaning on human understanding of Londyn's best placement; we never stopped to asked the Lord what He wanted.

Finally, we were at the point where we had no choice but to look in Little Rock because North Little Rock said, "NO, you cannot live here!" Don't you just love God? He literally closed every single possible door to get our attention and point us in the right direction. Yes, at the time this was so frustrating, but it taught me a lesson. The sooner we got to where He was, the doors flew open!

Had we insisted on North Little Rock, would He still be there? Of course, but He wants to always give us exceedingly and abundantly above what we can ask or think. In our own understanding, if we were denied in North Little Rock, there was no way we would get approved in Chenal. But we did! It was exactly where God wanted Londyn to be. She was zoned for Roberts, which was the best fit for her. Are there great schools in North Little Rock, of course! But her destiny was tied with West Little Rock.

Parent, thank and praise God for the closed doors. I am so glad we stopped and really focused on Him. Because of our obedience, Londyn and I have developed lifelong relationships with the staff at Roberts. Londyn has had the most wonderful educational experience there. Every word of our confession manifested. Londyn was at a great school where she met friends and had excellent teachers. Where she grew and helped others to grow.

He is so amazing and His timing is perfect. It was all part of His plan, and I will never doubt God's plan concerning Londyn.

She has always had the right doctors and therapists. We have been blessed with the right teachers; and even when challenges came, God stretched us which allowed maturity and growth. God is ordering her steps, but the key was to give her back to Him. I got out of the Holy Spirit's way so He can work for her good.

THE BIG TRANSITION

Unfortunately, many parents are misguided about the big transition. I am not here to endorse one particular setting. I just want you to stop and ask the Holy Spirit what is the best placement for your overcomer. I want to give you insight on my personal experience. I heard so much negativity centered on public schools. When we were deciding on the appropriate placement for Londyn, we were told that public school education would not be the best way to go. On countless occasions fellow parents would share their horrible experiences. The conclusion that seemed logical to me was Londyn needed to be in a private setting.

After realizing Little Rock School District was where He wanted us to go, it was time for me to get ready for their requirements. When I was preparing for our transition conference, I carried a lot of anger and most of it was not even mine. The advice that parents gave me was a broken record in my ears, which was taking root in my heart. This is dangerous. Lesson learned: Be mindful of what you allow your ears to hear and eyes to see. When you allow yourself to engage in anger, you are partnering with the consequences of that anger (Matthew 5:22).

That is why it is so important to ask the Holy Spirit to show you who can go with you on your journey. I am sure that those parents were only sharing with me the hurt that they had experienced. They were most likely justified in their frustrations with the schools. I know at times you are justified in your anger, but *He* wants you to bring it to *Him* for healing and the right results.

When the day finally came for our transition conference, I sat in the best seat in the house. My background as a school director, behavioral specialist, and classroom teacher could not compare to the seat that I would sit in, *the parent seat.* Londyn's entire team from North Hills made special arrangements to be there. It was also nice to see a familiar face on the other side of the table representing the school district.

INDIVIDUALIZED EDUCATION PROGRAM (IEP) MEETINGS AND CONFERENCES

Here is how I prepared:

1. I spent time in worship and prayer before going. This allowed the Holy Spirit the opportunity to have my full attention so that He could give me wisdom and insight.

2. I kept a binder. Londyn has a binder for every grade. This kept me organized and I could easily access anything that I needed. Helpful hint: I put my favorite picture of her in the sleeve of the binder. Seeing a glimpse of her smiling face encouraged me during the meetings.

3. Out of all of her meetings from kindergarten to fifth grade, I only went to one alone. Try not to go to any meeting alone until you are comfortable. Bring someone with you. This person may think of a question or comment that you have forgotten that needs to be answered. He or she can also take

notes, since most likely you will be overwhelmed. Londyn's great-granny, both grandmothers, and aunt Amy have attended several meetings. If a co-parent or family member cannot attend, ask a road trip buddy. This can include a church member, neighbor, coach, etc. Remember, you want someone the Holy Spirit has approved.

4. I developed a relationship with the team. The team leader, usually the counselor or the school-based special education department head, can assist you with informal introductions. I always emailed prior to the beginning of the school year and asked if I could stop by and introduce myself. This also gave me peace about the upcoming year.

5. If you have questions about setting up meetings or evaluations, ask your healthcare providers, school team, or local advocates.

6. I researched and became an expert. No one can advocate like you. Stay informed and current with policies.

7. Connect with local agencies and support groups. They have information that is not available to some providers.

8. Ask the Holy Spirit for a parent mentor you can look to for insight and guidance. They are great sounding boards for you to vent. They will not add fuel to the fire, but they will give you sound wisdom. I still get calls from my parent mentees, and I love it!

9. Read the fine print. It is important that you take time to read every document you receive. If there is something you do not understand, ask questions.

10. Make a list of your concerns to be addressed at the meeting.

Sometimes we want what is best for our comfort versus what is in the best interest of our children. I am talking about myself. Londyn was leaving a school with one hundred students and going to a school with nine hundred students. I had decided that I was not leaving the meeting without having an Instructional Aide added to her plan. The team made a decision that she did not need one, but they were sensitive to my request as a parent. The team was right. Londyn did not need the aide…period.

If you have concerns, alert the team leader ASAP. Please do not allow a concern to turn into worry and anger in your heart.

Let go of your pride. Release your need to be right or what you think is right. Remember, conversations that God has not led you to, will lead to poor decision making. Peace equals choosing battles wisely and remembering the battle is not yours, it's the Lord's (Exodus 14:14).

TO SELF-CONTAIN OR NOT SELF-CONTAIN

Londyn has always been mainstreamed into the general education population, while receiving additional support. I remember when we first walked into Londyn's elementary school. It was so big. There was no way that I would send my baby there. She would get lost. She would be invisible. The most powerful moment I remember is when Dr. Loudermill pulled me to the side. I know she could sense my fear and uneasiness. She said, "We are going to take care of your baby." Simple words that meant so much for me. Did these words give me permission to slack off? Of course not.

I understand the dilemma in deciding what is best: "Do I put my child in a smaller class with kiddos like her who also range in different diagnoses? Do I put her in an environment with more typical kids? But will she get lost or forgotten?" Both solutions are great. It is important for you to take a step back and do what is best for your child in the moment. A transition can take place if you find that it is not the right fit.

With Londyn's typical peers, she was mostly catered to. That can be a good or not-so-good situation. She would walk in a classroom and the kids would do everything for her. They loved helping her; and to be honest, sometimes they loved babying her.

They wanted to include her in everything they were doing. Sometimes what they wanted was lost in relation to what she understood. I remember explaining to her friends that she was not ignoring them, she was just in her own little world, which was appropriate wording for first graders.

Londyn did not believe she had friends at school. I alerted her team leader, Ms. Downing, who immediately developed a plan of action by observing Londyn during lunch and asking the Instructional Aides to be on the lookout. It is so important that you make your concerns known.

I remember taking her to school one day and thinking, *Lord I cannot reach that far, but You can.* I begin to pray out loud and I had Londyn repeat after me. "Lord, when I am alone, remind me that You are always with me!" Then the time came when she did not want anyone's help, even when she needed it. She was becoming more independent.

Friend, we spend way too much time trying to figure it out all by ourselves, when Jesus not only has "the answer" but *He is the Answer*. Every year, God has provided the provision that we needed. Testimony = He wants to do it again.

Steps to maintain positive relationships in your overcomer's learning environments:

1. Communication: Check in with the teachers weekly. Send a positive note or get to the school early enough to say "hello."

2. Be visible. We are given the schedule for events at the beginning of the year. Make plans to attend or send a friendly face. If her dad or I could not go, we sent my mama or Aunt Amy.

3. Invite her teachers to out-of-school activities. This continues to build relationships.

4. Take ownership of their education. Although the school has responsibility, we ultimately are responsible.

5. A child cannot be successful where they are not valued. You absolutely do not have to stay in an unhealthy situation. The Holy Spirit will show you.

6. Our commute to school always included worship and empowerment songs. I wanted Jesus on her mind as she entered the school.

7. Being proactive is wise versus being reactive. There are moments when you will be justified in your response. Take a deep breath before calling, meeting,

sending a text, or email. Share any decisions with your road trip buddy before doing anything.

8. I told Londyn she was the smartest in her school. We always rehearse in our minds our perceptions of ourselves, so I wanted her perception to be positive and give her confidence.

9. And when she does not understand, I tell her to lean not on her own understanding and to remember she can always ask Jesus for help.

10. Remind them daily that they are never alone. Jesus is always with them.

As mentioned before, when we had our initial transition conference from preschool to public, I came prepared with my mom-game on. I was ready for a fight when God already had it all worked out for our good. Your case may have not been as pleasant. I want you to utilize your resources. Contact your local advocacy and disability rights agencies.

Every parent wants their child to be successful. It should not be based on a lottery system where a few kids get lucky every once in a while. It is their birthright. Children are His heritage. My heart hurts after receiving the many calls from parents and guardians wanting more for their kids. I know that there are great educators who want it too. I want to minister hope to you. From now on, I stand in agreement with you that you will have a great experience. Your child *will* be successful, a genius!

We have been so blessed. I want you to pray and ask God for His plan for your child's life. He knows it, and He wants the best for your overcomer more than we ever could.

NOW TAKE AUTHORITY

Pray: "Lord, Your goodness, mercy, and unfailing love will follow _____ (Psalm 23:6). _____ has strength for all things in Christ who empowers _____. _____is ready for anything and equal to anything through Him who infuses inner strength into my child. _____ is self-sufficient in Christ's sufficiency (Philippians 4:13)."

We partnered with wisdom by declaring James 1:5 (NCV) *"But if any of you needs wisdom, you should ask God for it. He is generous to everyone and will give you wisdom without criticizing you."*

Write: "God, give me wisdom" on a post-it note and hang it in a place where you will see and speak it daily.

The following is the confession I wrote before Londyn started kindergarten. Stand on Job 22:28.

2013 Confession

> Londyn will be enrolled in a school today that she will love and enjoy. Where she can grow and help others to grow. Her school will be surrounded by God-fearing people who are Holy Spirit filled and who do not operate unless they consult the Holy Spirit first. She will excel academically. She will improve her speech, language development, motor skills, and anything that is lacking in her body today!! She will have favor among all the teachers, staff, administrators, parents, students, therapists, and anyone who comes in contact with her! They will always want only the best for her and will ALWAYS have her best interest at heart. Everyone who comes in contact with Londyn will always make her education and

well-being their priority. I thank You for the aide that You are raising up for Londyn. I praise God that she will be an advocate for Londyn; she will LOVE to come to work and will believe she is fortunate and blessed to have Londyn as her student. She will cover Londyn and make Londyn's education and well-being her priority.

It is time for you to write your own confession:

_____

_____

_____

_____

_____

_____

_____

_____

Not only is it important in their earthly learning, but learning the things of God is the most important lesson you can ever teach them. Their own daily devotion will spark the hunger within them. There are many great devotionals that can be purchased or are available on Bible apps. If they cannot read on their own, read it to them.

FAITH IN ACTION

Develop a close relationship with their teacher. During the school year, your overcomer spends more time during the day with them than you do.

Research what can be added to their 504 and IEP, for example, special seating.

A buddy program: Ask the Holy Spirit to highlight a student who could be your child's buddy. Londyn and Gauri were buddies first to fifth grade. With her mom's permission, the school placed them in the same class. Not only did Londyn get the benefits of having someone she could lean on, Gauri was able to "exercise/show" leadership and servanthood.

Introduction: Provide awareness of your overcomer's personality and learning style. This will prepare their peers and also educate them on social cues.

Plan for their future and write down their visons. Ask them what they want to be when they grow up, and refer to them as Doctor, Nurse, Officer, Teacher, etc.

Remember, children are fruit from our trees. If they are struggling in any specific area, ask the Holy Spirit if they are mimicking anything that you are struggling with.

Standardized testing: The week of the test, we rested in His peace; God knew the plans for Londyn's life, and a test cannot and will not define it. When she came to a question she did not understand, I told her to repeat these words: "Jesus, please help me select the right answer."

SCRIPTURES TO STAND ON

Lord, I remember what you have done. I remember the amazing things you did long ago. I think about those things. I think about them all the time (**Psalm 77:11-12**).

Before you do anything, put your trust totally in God and not in yourself. Then every plan you make will succeed (**Proverbs 16:3 TPT**).

Teach them to obey everything that I have taught you, and I will be with you always, even until the end of this age (**Matthew 28:20 NCV**).

You will not have to do anything but stay calm. The Lord will do the fighting for you (**Exodus 14:14**).

He said, "Listen to me, King Jehoshaphat and all you people living in Judah and Jerusalem. The Lord says this to you: "Don't be afraid or discouraged because of this large army. The battle is not your battle, it is God's"' (**2 Chronicles 20:15 NCV**).

When you are angry, don't let that anger make you sin, and don't stay angry all day (**Ephesians 4:26**).

OVERCOME YOUR ENVIRONMENTS

My people will dwell in a peaceful habitation, in secure dwellings, and in quiet resting places.
—Isaiah 32:18 NKJV

I decided long ago that there must be peace in my home. No matter how our day went and the giants we faced, home was where we rested. Home is where anointing oil spots are reminders where we've taken authority in various places. It is where we are constantly reminded of God's love by the many post-it notes covering our walls in every room. We put a demand in our home that its testimony would be Isaiah 32:18.

Autism loves to encourage chaos. I will not blame autism for every stressed moment, but I will admit that it is an easy scapegoat. Autism forces you to believe that your life is supposed to look like uncertainty, stress, and chaos. That our home and everywhere we went the atmosphere would change because of it. We refused to believe the lie. We declared that we were built on an unshakable foundation. A foundation that no matter what storm came, we stood strong because of it. Not only do our feet rest on a Firm Foundation, but our home was built on the same Unshakable Foundation—God's Holy Word.

We stood on Matthew 7:24-25 (TPT) and confessed it over our lives:

> *Everyone who hears my teaching and applies it to his life can be compared to a wise man who built his house on an unshakable foundation. When the rains fell and the flood came, with fierce winds beating upon his house, it stood firm because of its strong foundation.*

The key is to not only *hear* His teachings, but to also *apply* the teachings to your lives.

I love watching nature shows. I enjoy each program and watching God's beautiful creation. It amazes me how animals adapt to their environments. The snow fox is white in the winter and not easy to spot against the beautiful white snow. When summer comes, its fur is brown, the same color that appears as the snow melts.

We are the same. We survive and adapt to our environment. If we are not careful, we will conform to unhealthy environments. This is why we must seek the Holy Spirit in all we do. Some environments appear healthy when they are not. I am sure a baby gazelle sees beautiful green grass, not realizing there is a lion hiding and waiting to pounce.

Peace is so important for our overcomers. There are places where Londyn and I did not go because of their lack of peace. I am in awe of how Londyn is very sensitive to her surroundings. This is a blessing, but also has its challenges. I knew when something was off by the way she reacted. Her echolalia would get louder and faster. Her eyes would turn all around in her head. It caused me to be more prepared and aware of her surroundings. This began in our home.

Our home had to be her safe haven. In public, especially at school, she had to quiet her echolalia, stimming, and her more physical behaviors. I did not want her to quiet them, I wanted her to take authority over them. She reacted to the changes in this matter to feel safe and free. Autism wanted chaos and irritability; and if you allow it, there is no peace. I did an atmosphere detox. Our spiritual bodies are like gas tanks. It is up to us to fill it with the right fuel. By allowing the Holy Spirit to lead me, He showed me what to allow in my home. I am not talking about being "too religious," I am talking about a spiritual balance. Let's be honest, whatever our spirits absorb will come out!

I want Londyn to have more of Jesus so that He will show up more in her actions. Most importantly, I want her to know her own Jesus and not Mommy's Jesus. We have to lead them to their own personal relationship and appreciation for Him. I want her heart to be connected to His and not for her to just repeat my actions or words that I say.

Did it mean that there were certain times I did not allow her to listen to secular music? Yes. Did I completely restrict secular music? No, but I always had her spiritual tank in mind. Secular music can lift, but Kingdom music nourishes her soul. Because kids on the spectrum usually give us cues to what mood they are in or how they are feeling, I would have worship music playing in the background. I made this observation. When Londyn is outside of our home, I am not there to see her minute-by-minute movements. When we are home, I made a point to keep an atmosphere of peace.

"How do you do that, Angeletta?" Simply put—I wanted peace, so I went to the Prince of Peace.

Tips for a positive environment:

1. Ask the Prince of Peace, Jesus, to show you what is stealing your peace and your overcomer's peace. Hint: The answer will not just be autism. It may be a friendship that needs His attention or what you have allowed to take root in your heart that He wants to heal.
2. While praying over your family, walk into every room in your house. Be on the lookout for anything in each room that may not be healthy for them.
3. Lay hands on your family and pray, especially while they sleep.
4. Play light worship music throughout the house.
5. Play any Bible app Scriptures while they sleep. Their spirits will be nourished constantly.
6. Say this out loud: "There will be peace in my home. Jesus, Your blood shields our home and shields us wherever we go."
7. Gather your road trip crew to come over, pray, and anoint your house with olive oil.
8. When you know you are about to be in a potentially stressful situation, try not to avoid it; rather, take authority over it by declaring #6 and confessing His Word over it.
9. I did not allow Londyn to be around negativity, especially in adults. With children, I am constantly training her the importance of acceptance and

building relationships. The Holy Spirit will direct you if you need to choose new friends and playmates for them.

10. Post confessions on paper throughout the house, so that whenever you enter the room you will remember to speak it in faith. I love catching Londyn reading them.

11. Make sure your village is on the same page.

12. Peace equals guarding your environment—stay vigilant, mindful, prayerful.

Whatever house you enter, first say, "Peace [that is, a blessing of well-being and prosperity, the favor of God] to this house" (Luke 10:5 AMP).

"Okay, Angeletta! I have commanded authority in my home. They will go to school tomorrow. Now what?"

When you have commanded authority in your life, it will follow your children wherever they go. When Londyn would get out of my car and walk into her school, I spoke this over her:

Londyn, the blood of Jesus covers you! Angels fight over you to protect you. Today will be your best day at school. God, lead the right people onto her path. Remove people who shouldn't be there. A blood shield surrounds this school and neighborhood. Angels, overcrowd this building. Londyn, you are the smartest kid at Roberts Elementary. You are blessed and highly favored among teachers, administrators, staff, students, parents, and visitors. They know that there is something special about you. God bless and keep you! I love you, honey.

YES! I prayed this prayer over her every day that I took her to school. The parents at the carpool line would say, "AMEN!"

We must stand guard. When something does not feel right, trust the God in you. Stop. Pray. Speak Psalm 91 over your household. I am very aware of Londyn's surroundings. Most importantly, angels are always surrounding her. Keep your confession before you. I am not saying that you have to recite so many times a day. God forbid if you skip a day!

As mentioned in Chapter 4, this is how I explained it to my mentees. I asked them, "How many times were you told that the sky was blue before you got to the point where you did not even think or question it? You just know that it is blue. It is the same as believing God's Word. The more you read and meditate on it; you will believe with all of your heart. It is your spiritual food that your body naturally craves."

WHILE AWAY FROM YOU

Co-parenting is not easy in general, but you have the Holy Spirit. He will show you how to get your child transitioned to their new reality. Practice and have everyone on board. Do not keep secrets from the village. When there is a tough transition at home, let teachers, therapists, pastors, etc., be aware so that they can cover you in prayer.

Spend time with the Holy Spirit first before speaking with a co-parent or guardian. Practice your conversation with Him. This will reveal what is really in your heart and what needs to come out. He will direct you, but most importantly, He will filter and show you your heart and mend it. When you do this, you will not have any regrets or think, *I wish I didn't say that.* Or, *I hate that I lost my cool.*

Sometimes what is best in our minds may not be best for our overcomers. The Holy Spirit will show you the right time and what to say. Try not to allow fear, doubt, or worry to take root in your heart. Remember, He cares about this and will not leave you without answers. Please do not keep secrets from your spiritual mentor. If you have decided to let it go, then do that. The more you think and talk about it, the more that little seed will grow, and grow, and grow into bitterness and resentment. Ask the Holy Spirit to show you how to honor them even when you don't think they deserve it. This is pleasing to God.

Because Londyn is in a co-parenting environment, I have learned the focus should never be on what the other parent is doing. I had to let go, and give her to Jesus. He can reach places I cannot. He is a way better Protector than I could ever be. Most importantly, I absolutely cannot control their decisions. I can only trust Him. Yes, it's not the greatest situation. But your child may be the light and example that will bring everyone closer to God. Tell your family and friends, in love, that you refuse to worry, but will stand on His Word:

> *What delight comes to the one who follows God's ways! He won't walk in step with the wicked, nor share the sinner's way, nor be found sitting in the scorner's seat. His pleasure and passion is remaining true to the Word of "I Am," meditating day and night in the true revelation of light. He will be standing firm like a flourishing tree planted by God's design, deeply rooted by the brooks of bliss, bearing fruit in every season of his life. He is never dry, never fainting, ever blessed, ever prosperous* (Psalm 1:1-3 TPT).

NOW TAKE AUTHORITY

Creating a peaceful, parental environment: One thing that I am most certain of—we can take authority in our environment. We can command peace to overwhelm us.

Remember, greater is He who is in you than he that is in the world. Confess this over yourself and your overcomer:

_____ is an atmosphere shifter because they carry Your presence, Lord God. When _____ walks in a room, people know that he/she belongs to You because _____ smells like You. _____ looks like You. _____ talks like You. _____ walks like You. Because Jesus lives in _____, no matter what the environment is, it will change hurt to healing, unloved to loved, doubt to certainty, and stress to peace.

In _____'s school he/she will find favor among the classmates, teachers, staff, parents, and visitors. They will know how special _____ is to You, Jesus.

While decreeing and declaring your confession, walk throughout your house. There will be peace wherever your feet land. Angels will go before you.

Write your thoughts after your walk-through.

FAITH IN ACTION

Behavior and environment go hand in hand. Your environment can impact your behavior, and your behavior can set the tone for the environment.

Take 5: Set your timer for five minutes. Put a worship song on repeat. Five is the number of grace and He wants you to receive. Say this, "Thank You, Lord. I am healed, free, and loved; I have peace." Before long you will crave more, want more, need more, and gotta have more time in His presence. When I gave God five minutes, I was able to write chapters. Imagine if we gave Him more and the opportunity for Him to personally recharge us. How much would we have?

Let's environmentally detox your home! Ask the Holy Spirit if there is anything in your home that is not good for your mind, body, or spirit. Specifically ask Him if there are any toys, movies, games, electronic apps, etc. that are not good. When He shows you the items, throw them away immediately. He has shown me what to block from Londyn's eyes and ears. You will see the changes after you obey the Holy Spirit. We are living witnesses. Do not be caught up in "I'm taking away the only thing that keeps them from having a meltdown" excuse. Trust the Holy Spirit and replace the items with whatever He shows you. I promise, He knows best and what He shows you will always be more satisfying than anything else.

Remember, if a co-parent still allows it in their home, do not worry or try to control their decisions. Be led by the Holy Spirit on how to speak with them about it. If they still allow it, remember, that Jesus is always with your overcomer. Pray over your child's mind, body, and spirit before he/she leaves your home. Because you have stepped into your authority, it will follow the child everywhere.

PULL OUT A CHAIR

He is a big God and can handle it. Here is a conversation that I had with Him recently. It may not make sense to you, but He understood me.

> *Lord, where is the answer? Londyn deserves better than this! I know I should be spending time in worship. I know I should turn off the TV and focus on You. I know I should be fasting. I'm all cried out. I'm tired. I know I should be at a prayer meeting. I feel good right now watching something funny. It can take my mind off of things temporarily. The problem is, I need the answer, and that television program is just not it. It gave me a temporary laugh. I need a lifelong teachable moment.*
>
> *The elders at Impact assured me that I was going in the right direction. Can I please get a sign? I mean a big sign, and not a little ole word, I need Heaven to part and a messenger be in my living room. I need a Gabriel sign that something big is about to happen. Can I please just get allocated for June? I need money! Can I please have one less thing to think about? Can You just go ahead and pay it? I know You can do it! Can you please answer me so I won't have to think about it? Okay, okay, I know. Trust You. But I need to be able to put the answer in the manuscript, so I'll need it before August 2019. Hello!! I have to tell the world that I am an overcomer.*

What a prayer—ha! It is okay if you feel like you can't get the words right. He understands you!

Your turn...

SCRIPTURES TO STAND ON

Go away! Leave me, all you troublemakers! For the Lord has turned to listen to my thunderous cry **(Psalm 6:8 TPT)**.

You, Lord, give true peace to those who depend on you, because they trust you **(Isaiah 26:3 NCV)**.

Now therefore, let it please You to bless the house of Your servant, that it may continue before You forever; for You, O Lord God, have spoken it, and with Your blessing let the house of Your servant be blessed forever **(2 Samuel 7:29 NKJV)**.

Through wisdom a house is built, and by understanding it is established; by knowledge the rooms are filled with all precious and pleasant riches **(Proverbs 24:3-4 NKJV)**.

Every house is built by someone, but God is the Designer and Builder of all things **(Hebrews 3:4 TPT)**.

You can go to God Most High to hide. You can go to God All-Powerful for protection. I say to the Lord, "You are my place of safety, my fortress. My God, I trust in you." God will save you from hidden dangers and from deadly diseases. You can go to him for protection. He will cover you like a bird spreading its wings over its babies. You can trust him to surround and protect you like a shield. You will have nothing to fear at night and no need to be afraid of enemy arrows during the day. You will have no fear of diseases that come in the dark or terrible suffering that comes at noon. A thousand people may fall dead at your side or ten thousand right beside you, but nothing bad will happen to you!

All you will have to do is watch, and you will see that the wicked are punished. You trust in the Lord for protection. You have made God Most High your place of safety. So nothing bad will happen to you. No diseases will come near your home. He will command his angels to protect you wherever you go. Their hands will catch you so that you will not hit your foot on a rock. You will have power to trample on lions and poisonous snakes. The Lord says, "If someone trusts me, I will save them. I will protect my followers who call to me for help. When my followers call to me, I will answer them. I will be with them when they are in trouble. I will rescue them and honor them. I will give my followers a long life and show them my power to save." **(Psalm 91)**

Encouragement for Caregivers, Family, and Friends

Autism is only a diagnosis, not my DNA. Not my identity! My identity is in Jesus. The song that I am about to sing sums it all up…I'm a child of God, yes I am!

—Londyn, age 11

A relational journey is about two or more people coming together for unity and purpose. This chapter is to encourage providers and caregivers who want to support their families, clients, patients, and friends.

Londyn and I appreciate you. We know that you have had to be brave through tough conversations. We also are aware that you regret giving your opinions, although perceived as speaking out of turn, when you thought it was best. Perhaps, getting the diagnosis was just as hard for you, but you did not know how to communicate your feelings for fear that you would seem inconsiderate of the other's feelings.

Not only have I had the privilege and honor to mentor many families, I have also given insight to educators, pastors, friends, and healthcare providers on how to build relationships and support families. Most recently I co-led a webinar for medical students with Dr. Bellando. The best way to share this is to walk you through my journey with Londyn's doctors.

In the chapter "Adios Diagnose," I shared my journey from the "dark diagnosing room" up to our beginning. I saved the best part until now. Londyn's doctors have always been on the road trip with us. Because autism is very complex, we could not just be assigned to any doctor. We prayed that God would link us up with the right doctor…and He did.

Let me be honest with you. Most parents cringe when they hear someone say something like, "My nephew has autism, so I understand." "I have worked with kids on the autism spectrum for years, so I know." I am not invalidating your experience. Just realize that every experience will always be very different. There is definitely no cookie-cutter intervention that will work for everyone.

It takes at least two individuals to make this work. I do not want you to think that the weight of the responsibility is on you to meet the need of the family directly impacted, without having any input. We as parents have a responsibility. We need to be clear about our needs and not have expectations in our minds that have not been communicated. Together let us close the lack of communication and relationship gap. I want to encourage those who want to understand more how to be a better teacher, youth/children pastor, neighbor, friend, and bonus parent.

The following are some ways that I have encouraged many to be successful and build relationships:

Be like the Holy Spirit in John 14:26 (AMP) *"But the Helper (Comforter, Advocate, Intercessor—Counselor, Strengthener, Standby)...."*

- Comforter: Do not add fuel to the fire. This will subject them to anger and fear. Offer support.
- Counselor: Be honest. Give all sides to the argument. This way will only make room for growth.
- Helper: Ask how you can help, don't decide that you know what the help is.
- Intercessor: Pray; this is most important. Please do not just say you will do it. Stop in that moment and *just do it*.
- Advocate: Even if you are not personally impacted by autism you need to know how to intercede.
- Strengthener: Strengthen with words of comfort; and most importantly, the Living Word of God.
- Standby: By spending time with the Holy Spirit, you will be ready and equipped to edify when you are needed.

Always before you begin your approach, which can be phone calls, face to face, etc.,...pray! Take a deep breath and release your need to be right. Be sensitive to the Holy Spirit. If you approach someone at the wrong time, you will build a wall between you and the person or persons. Establish trust by just listening. You really do not always have to speak. Remember, the heart of the Father is always reconciliation. Jesus gave specific instructions in Matthew 18:15-16.

FAMILIES AND CAREGIVERS

1. Be like Jesus in John 8:6,8: Stoop down and meet them where they are.

2. Be patient with them while they are processing the initial shock of the diagnosis. Ask the Holy Spirit to search your heart and show you how to be moved by patience, compassion, and lovingkindness.

3. It is not rare for a caregiver to feel helpless due to the lack of understanding of what the person closest to you is experiencing because of autism.

4. You can always vent to God and ask for help in processing your feelings. I remember when my mom and I had a conversation about her role as grandma after Londyn's diagnosis. Because the focus was on my feelings, she did not get the opportunity to process hers.

5. Set aside time just for them.

6. As a caregiver, when offering help, here is a tip that I have always found helpful. Ask: "What can I do for you?" rather than, "Do you need anything?" Or ask them their list of needs for the week and offer assistance with the tasks.

7. Plant seeds of love, joy, peace, patience, kindness, goodness, faithfulness, gentleness, and self-control, while realizing you may not get to see the harvest. Someone else will come along and cultivate what you have planted. There are so many trees on my family's land that our elders planted

many years ago but did not get to see them mature. Because of their seeds, our family can enjoy the beauty.

8. The Holy Spirit does not want you to judge, He wants you to intercede.

9. Your thoughts are just as loud as your words, yet you can pray without a person knowing.

10. Ask the Holy Spirit when to go and minister, so that you will have their attention.

FRIENDS

1. Check on your friends. Take them out. I know you mean well, but please stop saying, "If you need anything, call." Nine times out of ten, they will never call.

2. If there is a feeling in your heart to do something, be led by the Holy Spirit and do it.

3. Keep your word. Sure, I know stuff comes up and you have your own life. But if you say you are going to show up, show up.

4. Hold off on your feelings and advice until you ask the Holy Spirit for wisdom on when to express them. Practice what you want to say to them with the Holy Spirit first. This will help with your emotions.

5. Be guided by the beautiful friendship story in Luke 5:18-20; by any means, get them to Jesus.

PROVIDERS

1. Facilitate parent focus groups or boards with the intent of empowerment. You will be able to hear their needs and then they will in turn go out and encourage more parents to come to your organization.
2. Remind parents that you value them and their input. They need to be heard and validated in their feelings before you begin talking in scientific and technical terms.
3. My relationship with Londyn's pediatrician and developmental pediatrician has always been positive. Because they would be giving crucial information concerning Londyn's well-being, it was important that we connected.
   a. I was never just another appointment to them. They spoke directly to me and Londyn. She was never invisible. They asked her questions directly.
   b. All of my concerns were taken seriously.
   c. Her doctors did not hide behind a laptop or notes. We spoke at eye level like two human beings sharing information; there was never a superior tone.
   d. I never felt rushed.
   e. Her doctors treated my information as valuable and they always reminded me that I was so important to Londyn's care.
   f. They constantly validated me as Londyn's best advocate.

GOD WILL HELP YOU

Psalm 139:13-14 (NLT) says:

> *You made all the delicate, inner parts of my body and knit me together in my mother's womb. Thank you for making me so wonderfully complex! Your workmanship is marvelous—how well I know it.*

These summers have been *hot*. Not only just the weather, but our country has faced some fiery challenges. What I so love about our God is that He is very active and in tune with our everyday lives. There are some things in this world that we will never be able to control. What we *can* do is ask Him to search our hearts. As long as our hearts are turned toward Him, we have the Mender of broken hearts in control. We have a very present God who is very concerned about every aspect of our lives.

He is the God who says in Luke 12:7 (NLT) *"And even the very hairs of your head are all numbered. So do not be afraid; you are more valuable to God than a whole flock of sparrows."* Our God cares about every strand of hair on our heads! Think about it! Hair sheds, has split ends, and breaks off all day long, yet He keeps up with the accurate number? He cares for us!

If you have asked yourself during a parent's cry for help, *What can I do Lord?* in the midst of uncertainty, hurt, and pain—know that you can always pray. The Bible teaches us in Philippians 4:6-7 (NCV)

> *Do not worry about anything, but pray and ask God for everything you need, always giving thanks. And God's peace, which is so great we cannot understand it, will keep your hearts and minds in Christ Jesus.*

Even if we cannot "see" that our prayers are being answered, God is still working behind the scenes. Aren't you glad that the "distance" is from our eyes and ears, to our hearts?

REMIND YOUR OVERCOMER THAT GOD IS THE SOURCE

And my God shall supply all your need according His riches in glory by Christ Jesus (Philippians 4:19 NKJV).

Bills, bills, bills: Everyone has them! I know I am not alone when recalling moments where I have struggled because of bills, bills, bills. I am so glad that our God is very concerned about our lives, needs, and yes, bills! Second Kings 4 tells of a widow woman with an incredible story. She tells the prophet Elisha that bill collectors are coming to collect on her outstanding debts by taking her two sons as payment.

Have you had a bill collector call to demand payment on any outstanding debt? Were you able to pay? Here in the story, the widow woman did not have money to offer the bill collectors. In verse 2 Elisha asked her, "What do you have?" So I ask you today, "What do *you* have?"

See, I am not ashamed to say that I have been in the exact same place as the widow. Praise God they could not come and take my Londyn, but they could take very needed material possessions! At those times, I didn't even have oil (see verse 2); but what I did have was…me. I want to remind you that we have the True and Living God who has riches, glory, and wants His children to have it all. All He needs from us is our time, our worries, and our cares. His Word says in First Peter 5:7 (NLT), *"Give all your worries to God, for he cares about you."*

When we are focused on Him and not the bill, our faith gets stronger which allows God to move on our behalf. So say to your bills, bills, bills, "My God will meet ALL of my needs according to His riches and glory through Christ Jesus!"

GOD WILL DEFEND YOU

Psalm 91:11-12 (NLT) says, *"For he will order his angels to protect you wherever you go. They will hold you up with their hands so you won't even hurt your foot on a stone."* Fear. It cripples and causes us to hide in our feelings and pain. When fear is present, it causes us to make quick decisions that hurt more than help. But we have the victor over fear—His name is Jesus. At the beginning of Psalm 91, it reads, *"Those who live in the shelter of the Most High will find rest in the shadow of the Almighty."*

When we are in the shelter of God, who can hurt us? This is what we have to do to fear: *"This I declare about the Lord: he alone is my refuge, my place of safety; he is my God, and I trust Him"* (Psalm 91:2 NLT). We have to tell fear that our Lord is our refuge and safety, and we trust Him!

The next two verses proclaim: *"For he will rescue you from every trap and protect you from deadly disease. He will cover you with his feathers. He will shelter you with his wings. His faithful promises are your armor and protection"* (Psalm 91:3-4 NLT).

What a mighty God we serve! I challenge you to write this on a post-it note, and put it in your bathroom, kitchen, and or car: *"My Lord is my refuge and safety. I trust HIM!"* So every time fear tries to make a guest appearance, there is a constant reminder that he is not invited.

"If you make the Lord your refuge, if you make the Most High your shelter, no evil will conquer you; no plague will come near your home" (Psalm 91:9-10). Read Psalm 91 in its entirety daily. It is our Psalm of protection. It's God's personal way of saying, "I'll be watching you with love."

I'LL SAY A PRAYER FOR YOU

Colossians 1:11-12 (NLT) says:

We also pray that you will be strengthened with all his glorious power so you will have all the endurance and patience you need. May you be filled with joy, always thanking the Father. He has enabled you to share in the inheritance that belongs to his people, who live in the light.

Life can be very hard at times. Frankly, crawling in a dark hole and giving up, seems to be the best solution to our problems. But in life, the more we shut down, isolate ourselves, and pretend that nothing's wrong, the more likely our problems will get worse.

My friend, as you are reading, reflect on *"He has enabled you to share in the inheritance…."* When Christ ascended into Heaven, He left righteousness, peace, and joy as part of our inheritance. He also left a family of believers who pray for you daily. YES! I may not know you personally, but as Paul wrote in this letter, I pray that you, my friend, are strengthened in the Lord. I pray that you are reminded that nothing is too hard for God (Jeremiah 32:27). I also pray that you know that God is for you (Romans 8:31). So tonight, do not worry! Before I go to bed, I'll say a little prayer for you. Please pray for me and Londyn too.

CONFESSION

I speak the commanded blessings over myself and my household now in the name of Jesus! I am blessed. I am whole. I am healed from the crown of my head to the soles of my feet! My health springs forth like the morning. He satisfies my mouth with good things. With long life, the Lord will satisfy me and show me His salvation. I shall not die but live to declare the works of the Lord. I speak against any stronghold, curse, burden, or any assignment by the enemy…he is DEFEATED! I do the work of the ministry with a joyful heart. I am wise—the wisdom of God is within me. I am a soul winner! I lead others to the Cross where they are changed forever.

My mind is sound and renewed by the Word of God. I am not crazy! My thoughts are clear and I am not confused. I am empowered to prosper. I am prosperous in every area of my life—spirit, soul, and body. I am not rejected or forgotten. I am the head and not the tail. I am preferred and considered first. I am above only and not beneath! I am blessed in the city, in the town, in my state and the nation. My storehouses are full and my cup runs over. I decree this in my life—increase, increase, increase! Everything I put my hands to prospers. It flourishes.

I command life to spring forth. I speak a fresh anointing upon my life—fresh fire—fresh winds blow *now!* I declare that I shall have abundance in my life. I am fruitful in every area of my life and ministry! Promotions come! Business ideas come! Witty inventions come! A fresh anointing comes! I call forth every gift, talent, and ability within to manifest NOW in JESUS' name! I am lengthening my cords and strengthening my stakes. I STRETCH AND BREAK FORTH NOW IN THE NAME OF JESUS! THE BLESSING IS UPON ME, MY FAMILY, AND MY HOUSE!

HOMEWORK

Write a letter to a patient, caregiver, relative, provider, or teacher. You may choose to throw it away or give it to them. I encourage writing to help you release, but be led by the Holy Spirit before sharing it.

I love you, friend! Our love story to you, *Take Authority Over Autism* is only the beginning of our journey with you.

Remember: Seed. Time. Harvest. It's going to take greater faith, but it is worth it. Speak His Word over every situation in your life.

> *Oh, Lord God, you made the skies and the earth with your very great power. There is nothing too hard for you to do* (Jeremiah 32:17 NCV).

Watch out for blockers—dishonor, disobedience, anger, bitterness, and anything opposite of the fruits of His Spirit— that hinder us from receiving (see Galatians 5: 22-23).

> *A thief comes to steal and kill and destroy, but I [Jesus] came to give life—life in all its fullness* (John 10:10 NCV).

Love is the key. We want acceptance, but we are not accepting—He will help you. Simply pray: "Lord, teach me how to love like You love, and see Your people like You see them."

Speak blessings over your children daily. Make fun memories with them, reminding them that it is okay to be a kid.

Use God's words as a weapon, not your words. If there is anything that wants to hold you captive—your past, negative thoughts toward yourself and your family, persecution, guilt, shame, anger—worship until the prison walls come down! (See Acts 16:23-30.)

SCRIPTURES TO STAND ON

For God, the Faithful One, is not unfair. How can he forget the work you have done for him? He remembers the love you demonstrate as you continually serve his beloved ones for the glory of his name **(Hebrews 6:10 TPT).**

Love each other like brothers and sisters. Give each other more honor than you want for yourselves **(Romans 12:10 NCV).**

Be gentle with one another, sensitive. Forgive one another as quickly and thoroughly as God in Christ forgave you **(Ephesians 4:32 MSG).**

So speak encouraging words to one another. Build up hope so you'll all be together in this, no one left out, no one left behind. I know you're already doing this; just keep on doing it **(1 Thessalonians 5:11 MSG).**

So let's not allow ourselves to get fatigued doing good. At the right time we will harvest a good crop if we don't give up, or quit. Right now, therefore, every time we get the chance, let us work for the benefit of all, starting with the people closest to us in the community of faith **(Galatians 6:9-10 MSG).**

A gentle answer will calm a person's anger, but an unkind answer will cause more anger **(Proverbs 15:1 NCV).**

Abandon every display of selfishness. Possess a greater concern for what matters to others instead of your own interests **(Philippians 2:4 TPT).**

Help each other with your troubles. When you do this, you are obeying the law of Christ **(Galatians 6:2).**

If your brother or sister in God's family does something wrong, go and tell them what they did wrong. Do this when you are alone with them. If they listen to you, then you have helped them to be your brother or sister again **(Matthew 18:15)**.

Glossary of Terms and Acronyms

ASD: Autism Spectrum Disorder

Assistive technology device: tool used to assist individuals as they develop speech, including real-time speech-to-text transcription and visual recognition tools

Discernment: ability to judge well

Echolalia: unsolicited repetition of vocalizations made by another person

IEP: Individualized Education Plan

Preverbal: sounds that occur before the development of speech

Prophecy: message from God communicated by an individual giving inspiration, interpretation, or revelation

Prophetic activation: spiritual exercises that prompt prophetic gifts

Stimming: repetition of physical movements, sounds, words, or moving objects

299 Diagnosis code: autistic disorder, current or active state

Versions of the Bible used throughout (also see copyright page):

- Easy Read Version (ERV)
- New Century Version (NCV)
- The Passion Translation (TPT)
- New King James Version (NKJV)
- Amplified Version (AMP)
- The Message Bible (MSG)
- New Living Translation (NLT)

About the Author

Angeletta Giles' greatest accomplishment is being mom to Londyn, who was diagnosed with autism in 2012. Since then, Angeletta founded PAAK—Parent Advocates for Awesome Kids, where she has mentored and empowered parents worldwide. Their journey has been featured in publications for Autism Speaks, Savvy Magazine, and Arkansas Children's Hospital. Angeletta and Londyn live in Little Rock, Arkansas, with their dog, Cody.

Experience a personal revival!

Spirit-empowered content from today's top Christian authors delivered directly to your inbox.

Join today!
lovetoreadclub.com

Inspiring Articles
Powerful Video Teaching
Resources for Revival

Get all of this and so much more, e-mailed to you twice weekly!

LOVE TO READ CLUB

by **D** DESTINY IMAGE

www.ingramcontent.com/pod-product-compliance
Ingram Content Group UK Ltd.
Pitfield, Milton Keynes, MK11 3LW, UK
UKHW021312180426
11947UKWH00015B/1175